Here's what people are saying about

Life Skills:
Improve the Quality of Your Life with Metapsychology:

"This is the first time I read about Applied Metapsychology in clinical practice. I am lucky to have come across a concise, eminently-readable, empathic, joy-filled, hands-on text. Replete with examples, exercises, episodes from the author's life, and tips - this is a must for therapists (the book uses a much more benign term: "facilitators"), clients, and anyone who seeks heightened emotional welfare - or merely to recover from a trauma."
—Sam Vaknin, Ph.D., author of "Malignant Self Love: Narcissism Revisited"

"Marian K. Volkman's *Life Skills* is a serious, impressive, and thoughtful work with one objective in mind: teaching how to reach one's full potential in practical, pragmatic, easy-to-follow steps that will literally change one's life. This masterpiece of a survival guide will benefit all who turn its pages. The chapter on the importance of relationships is worth the price of the book alone, as most problems in life are relationship-oriented." —James W. Clifton, M.S., Ph.D., LCSW

"*Life Skills* by Marian Volkman is not to be read once and then put away. It is a guide to living a full, satisfactory life, a philosophy, a challenge. If you take the trouble to do the exercises the way the author suggests, they *will* change your life. When I edit a book, I look at words, sentences, and the way ideas are expressed and related to each other. With this book, I continually found myself thinking about the meanings the author discussed, relating them to my own experience, applying them to my own life. I think this shows the book's power. As a psychologist, I know that my work will have been improved through my reading of Life Skills." — Robert Rich, M.Sc., Ph.D., M.A.P.S., A.A.S.H.

D0911611

"There are books for reading and then there are books for studying. This is one of the latter, and is worth studying by everyone who would like to live more happily. It offers insights into the relatively new science of Metapsychology developed by Frank A. Gerbode M.D., an American psychiatrist whose university qualifications are sufficient to share around three or four eminent experts with a few to spare. He found a way to simplify the world view to its most basic, person-centred form and developed this into Metapsychology. Be warned, this book will probably affect the way you view everything and everyone around you. People who annoyed you previously will become more comprehensible, stressful situations will be less so and wise decisions will be easier to make. Most terrifying of all—you will be more likeable as you begin to like yourself more."

—Sue Phillips, Spiralthreads Reviews

"…This book will serve as a good resource for therapists, the general public will also find this book helpful. Topics are discussed in everyday language and explained without jargon or hidden superior attitudes. Furthermore, readers will find that the exercises that accompany each section of this book will not only help further solidify the concepts explained, but will also allow the reader to tailor his or her new findings to his or her life and particular situation. This aspect makes takes this book beyond just an excellent reference book of Metapsychological philosophies and techniques and brings these methodologies into the realm of self-help for all individuals wanting to improve the quality of their life."

—Tami Brady, Blether.com Reviews

"Volkman's primary objective in this volume is, as the subtitle suggests, to help improve the quality of her reader's life in all of its dimensions (mental, physical, emotional) by explaining various "Life Skills" which anyone can acquire and then strengthen. Volkman's ultimate objective is to help each reader to achieve maximum fulfillment of human potentialities, whatever the nature and extent of those potentialities may be."

—Bob Morris, Five-Star Reviews

Life Skills

Improve the Quality of Your Life
with Metapsychology

By Marian K. Volkman

First Edition: April 2005 (ISBN-13: 978-1-932690-05-7, ISBN-10: 1-932690-05-0)
Second Printing: August 2005

Publisher's Cataloging-in-Publication data
Volkman, Marian K.
Life skills : improve the quality of your life with metapsychology /   by Marian K. Volkman.
        p. cm.
        Includes bibliographical references and index.
        ISBN 1932690050
1. Self-help techniques--Problems, exercises, etc. 2. Change (psychology). 3. Psychoanalysis. I. Title.
BF637.B4 V65 2005
158.1 dc--22   2005901517

Available from: Baker & Taylor, Ingram Book Group, Quality Books, New Leaf Distributing.

Published by: Loving Healing Press
                  5145 Pontiac Trail
                  Ann Arbor, MI 48105
                  USA
http://www.LovingHealing.com or
info@LovingHealing.com
Fax +1 734 663 6861

Acknowledgements

The practical, useable tools in this book are based on the work of Frank Gerbode, M.D. Heartfelt thanks for all of the work and care to bring the subjects of Traumatic Incident Reduction and Applied Metapsychology into the world.

Many thanks go to the practitioners (facilitators) and trainers of these subjects who have shared their experience and knowledge with me over the years. Thanks also to my wonderful clients, for your courage, your insights and your willingness to share your experience with me.

Thanks also to my esteemed colleagues and fellow seekers in all subjects that aim to increase not only our understanding of human potential, but also to expand the apparent limits of that potential.

Thanks to my parents, Arie and Ellie Klopp, who started me out on the road to the exploration of human potential.

I owe a great debt of gratitude to writers who have informed and inspired me. A list of the books I mention herein appears in Appendix B.

Grateful thanks to Robert Rich, Ph.D. No one could ask for a wiser or more insightful editor. He is innocent of any oddities of language or punctuation that remain in this volume. They are mine alone.

Thanks to the people who were kind enough to critique various drafts: Victor Volkman, Stephanie Dreher and Jennifer MacLean.

Thanks to my assistant, Jake Coffin for doing so many things to help make writing possible.

Thanks to the following people for lending me space and quiet time to write (and in some cases computers and innumerable cups of tea): Suzanne Wilson, Henry Whitfield, and Steve and Frances Bisbey.

Thanks to the people of Landmark Education for their excellent work, especially Greg Hartman, Nitzana York, and Zanzibar Vermiglio.

Special thanks to my husband Victor, without whom this work would not have been finished any time soon!

Finally, thanks to my dear family, to whom I dedicate this book.

Explorations in Metapsychology Series:

- **Beyond Trauma: Conversations on TIR, 2ⁿᵈ Edition**
  Ed. by Victor R. Volkman

- **Life Skills: Improve the Quality of Your Life with Metapsychology** by Marian K. Volkman

- **Traumatic Incident Reduction: Research and Results** Ed. by Victor R. Volkman

- **AMI/TIRA Newsletter Volumes 1-2: Selected Reprints 2004-2005**, Ed. by Victor R. Volkman

- **TIR and Metapsychology Lecture Series**
  (MP3 CDs) with Frank A. Gerbode, M.D., et. al.

- **Traumatic Incident Reduction, 2ⁿᵈ Edition**
  by Gerald French and Chrys Harris, Ph.D.

Series Editor: Robert Rich, Ph.D.

*"To be what we are,
and to become what we are capable of becoming,
is the only end in life"*
—Robert Louis Stevenson (June 1880)

Loving Healing Press is dedicated to producing books about innovative and rapid therapies which redefine what is possible for healing the mind and spirit.

About our Series Editor, Robert Rich, Ph.D.

Loving Healing Press is pleased to announce Robert Rich, Ph.D. as Series Editor for the *Explorations in Metapsychology Series*. This exciting new series brings you the best of Metapsychology in practical application, theory, and self-help formats.

Robert Rich, M.Sc., Ph.D., M.A.P.S., A.A.S.H. is a highly experienced counseling psychologist. His web site www.anxietyanddepression-help.com is a storehouse of helpful information for people suffering from almost any way we can make ourselves and each other unhappy.

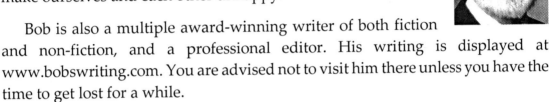

Bob is also a multiple award-winning writer of both fiction and non-fiction, and a professional editor. His writing is displayed at www.bobswriting.com. You are advised not to visit him there unless you have the time to get lost for a while.

Two of his books are tools for psychological self-help: *Anger and Anxiety: Be in Charge of your Emotions and Control Phobias* and *Personally Speaking: Single Session Email Therapy*. However, his philosophy and psychological knowledge come through in all his writing, which is perhaps why three of his books have won international awards, and he has won many minor prizes. Dr. Rich currently resides in Wombat Hollow in Australia.

About the Cover

The 3-D hands were designed by Fred Himebaugh (www.FredöSphere.com) using Imageware 12. This image was then layered with Hubble Space Telescope imagery of V838 Monocerotis (approx. 20,000 light years distant) as captured on 2/8/2004. Creative director for the cover design was Victor R. Volkman.

Table of Contents

Table of Figures

Introduction: How to Get the Most from this Book

This book provides you with some fundamental Life Skills for enhancing your abilities:

- To be fully present.
- To increase your knowledge and awareness of how life works.
- To bring about positive change in your mental and emotional world, which makes bringing about positive change in the outer environment much easier to do.
- To access more of your potential through practical exercises.

I personally detest books that tell me what to do, for example, books with suggested exercises that say something like: "Do everything in order," or, "Write everything down; don't just think about it." We all process information in our own ways. The exercises are suggestions only. I invite you to read and use this book in whatever way suits you best. Each time a word with a definition particular to this subject is used, it has been *italicized*, indicating that it is included in the glossary (see Appendix A).

The purpose of this book is to make all of these tools handily accessible for therapists and practitioners of all types, their clients, and people who wish to use them, either individually or in a group setting. This is the first book written with the purpose of making these tools available directly to the reader for use in daily life.

Life Skills is based on the practical use of concepts from *Applied Metapsychology*. While no one would claim that this subject contains everything you need to know about life, it does provide tools and strategies that I have found among the most useful I have ever encountered. I use the philosophy and methods of *Metapsychology* with my clients in one-on-one sessions. They come to me for a variety of reasons, because they are seeking: resolution and relief from traumatic experiences, better relationships, personal growth, more success, or increased awareness. Because my aim is to empower my clients as much as I can, I have taught the concepts and methods covered in this book to individuals for many years. In return, my clients have taught me much too. That is one of the reasons why I love this work, the continual opportunity for learning and insight. I invite you to explore these concepts, to try them on for size, and to see where they fit within your own wise understanding of life.

Because Metapsychology is *person-centered* in nature, you can incorporate these tools into your own frame of reference. What have you observed as being true? What works for you? I am much less interested in selling you on any of these ideas than I am in inviting you to think about all of these things and to draw your own conclusions.

Finally, I invite you also to consider taking the *TIR* (*Traumatic Incident Reduction*) and Metapsychology training, whether or not you have or want to have a career in the helping professions. There is a great deal to be gained from this training in terms of personal life skills. (For more details see www.tir.org and www. beyondtrauma.com.)

Use of this Book by a Reading or Study Group

Though any individual or any pair of people can effectively put the information and exercises presented here to work, this book is ideally suited to groups who read or study together. Group discussion always improves the depth of one's understanding of new material. After discussion the exercises can be done in pairs.

If you:

1. Ask each question of your partner.
2. Listen attentively to his/her answer (long or short).
3. Acknowledge that answer so that your partner knows that s/he has been heard and understood. (Something simple like, "Good" or "OK" or "All right" works best.)
4. Refrain from comment, judgment or interpretation.
5. Take each exercise to an end point of your partner feeling complete and satisfied.

…then you are doing facilitation

While there is a lot more to know about this subject, especially if you want to use it in a professional context, these techniques used in a personal growth context can be effective in promoting increased quality of life. When people work together like this, taking turns to do the exercises, we call it co-facilitation.

If a group were to study and practice all of this material, they would have a new set of skills, both as individuals and as a group.

If you like the idea of working this way but lack a handy group to work with, you have the option to start your own local study group. Another option is to join an online study group. To join, setup, or find an online study group, go to www.BookMovement.com and search for "Life Skills".

1 Quality of Life: What is Possible?

- What is Quality of Life? What is Possible in Terms of Human Potential?
- How Good Can Your Life Get?
- Is there Purpose to Our Existence and if So, What Is It?
- The Person-Centered Viewpoint
- Life as a Journey or School vs. Life as Art
- How do We Achieve and Maintain Our Potential?

This book offers tools that you can use to improve the quality of your own life, both immediately and as the on-going project that life is.

Exercise 1-1:

- **Either as a writing exercise, talking it over with another person, or just thinking about it, invent your own definition of quality of life.**
- **Are there things that cannot be present for quality of life to be good?**
- **Once you have achieved a good quality of life, how do you recognize it?**
- **How good can it get?**

Either by doing Exercise 1-1 or just thinking about it for a minute, take a look at your own ideas on the following: What makes life good? How good can it get: Emotionally? Mentally? Physically? In relation to others?

Fun, enjoyment, contentment, lightheartedness, pleasure, wonder, humor and delight must be part of the equation for the phrase "excellent quality of life" to apply.

Most of us would agree that adequate supplies of food, clothing and shelter are necessary as well for a reasonable quality of life. Until those basics are covered, people don't usually have much free attention to devote to such things as personal growth. People vary on how much money they consider to be necessary for life to be good, but most of us require a certain level of safety (in our homes, in our streets, in our environment and our economy), in order to feel that life is as it should be. Quality of relationships probably determines quality of life more surely than wealth does, once a certain minimum financial well-being is attained.

Maslow's well-known hierarchy of needs applies: Physiological needs such as food, clothing and shelter must be met first. The second need is for safety, then come our needs for society, esteem and finally actualization. Talking to a hungry person about personal growth or even trauma resolution is unlikely to meet the need that is uppermost. Once our basic survival needs are met we have attention and energy free to address the question of optimum quality of life.

How Good Can Your Life Get?

The question remains, given that every life has its ups and downs, how good can it get? Here is an inventory of components of high quality life that we can consider.

- **Daily Life:** If you wake up each morning eager for the day and what it will bring…

- **Physical Well-Being:** If you feel good in your body, comfortable in your skin; If you get far more pleasure from it than pain; If you delight in the sensations of ordinary things: warm water on your skin, comfortable clothing, cool morning air on your face…

- **Mental Well-Being:** If you feel good in your mind, feeling that it responds well to what you want it to do; If you delight in thinking, in working to understand new concepts and in playing with new ideas…

- **Spiritual Well-Being:** If you feel good in spirit: at peace with yourself and at home in the world; If you feel challenged and interested by the demands of life without being overwhelmed by them…

- **Daily Work:** If you have a good balance in your work and your play and find pleasure in both; If you are proud of what you produce in your daily work, and happy with the payment or exchange you get for what you do…

- **Relationships:** If you delight in the relationships you have with those around you, whether that includes a spouse, parents, children, neighbors, friends, co-workers, or chance-met strangers; If these relationships bring you far more pleasure than pain; If you delight in knowing these people and know that they delight in you…

- **Intimacy:** If you have, as Washington Post columnist Carolyn Hax puts it, "…the awareness that comfortable, loving, honest, seemingly bottomless intimacy is possible"…

- **Harmony:** If you feel in balance and harmony with the world such that your survival does not diminish the quality of life of others, but enhances it…

- **Learning:** If your life includes the stimulation of learning and personal development in whatever forms you choose: education (either formal or self-designed), physical and/or mental exercises, therapy perhaps, or religious observance, reading and conversation, so that new aspects of consciousness and awareness emerge to delight you…

- **Aesthetics:** If you seek out and enjoy beauty, not just in art and music, but in daily mundane scenes and objects; If you find aesthetic experience already existing all around you: a fresh loaf of bread, the color of bricks, the slant of evening light, a cloud, a bird, and you also consciously bring it into your life: a pretty table, a well-made meal, a collection of rocks or shells…

- **Nature:** If you delight in the wonder of the natural world in its richness, variety and ingenuity…

- **Your Identity:** If you feel good in yourself: in touch with your strengths and weaknesses, comfortable with your integrity, your creativity and your very being, at the same time willing to expand and develop all of your abilities as life flows on…

If all or most of these things are true, a person has an extraordinarily high quality of life. Notice how you feel, having read that list of possibilities. It can be depressing to contemplate the ideal and notice the disparity between what could be and what is. Since life involves effort, change and uncertainty, the above is more a picture of a theoretical ideal state than a standard one can never achieve. Instead, having a concept of the ideal gives us something to aim for, and something, hopefully, to inspire us.

> Quality of relationships determines quality
> of life more surely than wealth does.

Having What Is vs. Changing What Is

Two abilities have profound impact on our potential to optimize the quality of life:

- Our ability to fully enjoy and appreciate what is around us, what we already have.
- Our ability to change and adapt the actual conditions of our lives to suit ourselves.

Eastern philosophy tends to emphasize the former, Western the latter. In a well-known television series episode (you will recognize it if you have seen it), a Russian woman says to an American man, "You Americans are never happy. You have so much and yet you are never content." Well, yes. Dissatisfaction is built into a consumer-based society. Thinking of this, we can see that it truly is not only a skill, but a great richness to have the capacity to enjoy what is. The Emotional Scale (Chapter Three) bears on this, as do the effects of traumatic stress (Chapter Two). For now, let us just consider this as a pure ability.

Exercise 1-2:

- Depending on what appeals to you, go to an art museum, an antique auto show, a zoo, a public garden, a jewelry or department store, or any place where there is a large collection of things you especially like or want.
- To expand your ability to have and appreciate things without having to have legal title or physical possession of them, walk around choosing which things you most want to look at.
- One at a time, practice having them just where they are. Drink in their beauty and fine qualities. Decide that you can have them, just where they are.
- Do this as long as it interests you or until you feel a positive shift in your ability to have things without needing to own them.

Exercise 1-3:

For excellent practice in seeing, walk around with a camera, or pretend that you have a camera with you.

- Notice what you are looking at as if it were going to be recorded as a picture.
- Notice the quality of light: is it sharp or soft? Notice how high the sun rises in the sky at different times of the year.
- Notice composition, contrast, interestingly shaped objects, and interestingly shaped spaces.

Having What Is

The drive to possess things has fueled a great deal of human inventiveness and creativity. While we can acknowledge that, in *Reviving Ophelia* (1995), Pipher points out that this same drive can lead to people having, "houses full of junk, and no time." We can expand our capacity to *have* something beyond taking the thing home and putting it in our house or garden, where we admire it, paint it, or chop it up for firewood, as we choose. That is only one kind of having.

By enlarging the concept of possession, we can "have" a statue in a park and enjoy it fully, without feeling sad that we aren't allowed to take it home and install it in front of our own house. We can enjoy the possessions and furnishings of our friends with pure pleasure and no envy. We can enjoy the delightful qualities of another person's spouse without feeling the need to break up two families in order to fully "have" that person. Window shopping when we are feeling on top of the world can be a very pleasant exercise. Window shopping when we are feeling depressed merely adds another reason for depression – "Look at all those nice things that I can't possess."

After this examination of the ability to have desirable things, let's look at the ability to have things that we judge as less desirable. At this moment as I sit at my computer, I can look slightly to the right and see out a window. Perfectly framed in the window, which is a very tall Italianate style window with ancient wavy glass in it and a detailed wooden frame around it, is the stalk of a very tall stargazer lily, the buds still tightly furled and green. In front of the window is a nice old wooden chair that was my grandfather's, with a green seat in need of reupholstering. The cat likes to sit on this chair, but he can't at the moment because it is taken up by a set of files representing lots of work awaiting attention. Outside the window is a cold, gray July day. (July of course is usually one of the hottest and clearest months in Michigan.) The window is dirty.

Consider this picture with me for a moment if you will. What choices do we have here, without taking any action to change the physical environment? It would be easy to try and avoid anything in this picture which we might deem to be undesirable by projecting ourselves forward into the future, anticipating the glorious blooming of this lily plant (eleven buds!), hopefully with some sun to show off its rich color and bring out its enticing fragrance. It might be just as easy to feel that the lily is not worth looking at as it is now, before it blooms.

Even if we see the lily plant as beautiful as it is right in this moment, we might consider that the dirtiness of the window, the stack of files on the chair, or the gray, cold day, spoil our ability to appreciate it. Or, we might make a big effort to ignore what we don't like and appreciate the lily (or the chair, or the window itself) *in spite of* those things. Finally, we have the choice to take in the whole picture in the present and appreciate every bit of it, just as it is and each component as part of the whole.

This doesn't mean that we cannot wash the window if we choose to, or move the files, or light some candles to brighten the gloom; it just means that we don't have to do those things in order to have a good experience. If one has any lingering traces of the Puritan world-view that characterizes pleasure as sinful, the idea of working to develop one's capacity for enjoyment might seem like something wrong or at best, self-indulgent. I leave it to you to decide on that. The author Bill Bryson is extremely funny on the subject of how English people have the ability to squeeze every drop of pleasure from small comforts, and at the same time how willing they are to put up with discomforts others might consider intolerable.

If you decide that you'd like more capacity for pleasure, try Exercises 1-4 thru 1-6 on pp. 11-11.

Changing What Is

Now let's take a look at the other side of the equation, improving our quality of life by taking action to change the environment to suit ourselves. The positive side of a "This isn't good enough" attitude is the willingness to work to bring around positive change in the environment, at least from one person's point of view.

Exercise 1-4:

- **Look around your current environment and find something you can enjoy and appreciate, just as it is. Do this as long as you find it interesting or until something shifts in a positive direction for you.**
- **Repeat daily or as often as you like.**
- **Notice whether your ability to notice things improves over time.**
- **Notice whether you ability to enjoy what you notice improves.**
- **If you find this very hard, look for some aspect of each thing you notice, no matter how small an aspect, that you can appreciate, for example the grain of the wood in an otherwise ugly table.**

> Robert Rich, Ph.D. notes: "I used to uniformly dislike insects. Now I notice their beauty, enjoy their energy, and only kill those that attack me like mosquitoes and flies. I do go to some trouble to rescue one that is in danger."

Exercise 1-5:

- Think of a person who is so familiar to you that you hardly feel a need to look at him or her, someone whose habits and thoughts you know almost as well as your own.
- Really look at that person in a new moment and find some things to appreciate (in his or her looks, gestures, character, anything).
- Repeat daily or as often as you like.
- Notice whether your ability to notice things improves.
- Notice whether you ability to enjoy what you notice improves.
- Do this as long as you find it interesting or until something shifts in a positive direction.

Exercise 1-6:

If you like, do that last exercise with total strangers, especially with ones who do not particularly appeal to you.

Both abilities are essential for full, excellent quality of life:
the ability to appreciate what is, as it is,
and the ability to cause change

Effective change in our environment depends on first seeing what is so. Many of the exercises in this book can be used to increase your ability to do just that. This is not meant to make little of your abilities as they are now. Few if any of us could say that we are as in command of our abilities as we would like to be. Exercising those abilities develops them to new levels. Many of the exercises in this book empower you to more effectively change what is.

The Person-Centered Viewpoint

It's easy (and fun!) to judge other peoples' lives, choices, styles and habits. We can invest a lot of time into this and end up with not much to show for it at the end. Or we can take a page from psychologist Carl Rogers and try a different approach.

One of the things I like most about the work of Frank A. Gerbode, M.D., is that it is *person-centered*. When making use of Applied Metapsychology in one-on-one sessions, we call our practitioners *facilitators*, rather than counselors or therapists, so as to emphasize the idea that the practitioner's job is to bring about the safe time and space of the session for the client to do the important work. The facilitator provides structure and guidance to allow the client, whom we call the *viewer*, to look at various parts and components of his/her mental world. We can't get inside another person's mind. We can only ask him/her to look and tell us what s/he sees. In the process of *viewing*, things shift and change for the viewer as s/he reorders his/her mental world.

All of the exercises in this book are meant to be done from a person-centered point of view. If you do them on your own, try just brainstorming: acknowledging and being with your responses to the exercise, rather than criticizing or judging them. If you are doing the exercises in pairs or with a group, listen, understand and acknowledge what the other person says without judging it, to the best of your ability.

One can take a person-centered attitude toward life, not in the sense of being a doormat and letting other people have their way all of the time, but in the sense of accepting people as they are. Charlotte Davis Kasl (*If the Buddha Married*, 2001) recommends to married couples that they "abandon hope" of reforming their mates. Giving up the need to change other people (admittedly, not easily done) or their houses, possessions, appearance, choices, etc. has an immediate positive impact upon your quality of life, and theirs as well.

Exercise 1-7: Try for some period of time: 3 days, a week, or as long as you like, to do the following:

Every time you have a critical or negative thought about yourself or another:
1. **Notice it without judging it.**
2. **Acknowledge it for what it is.**
3. **Let it go.**

Notice what results you get from doing this.

Life as a School vs. Life as Art

Let us consider two possible cosmic viewpoints on the purpose or meaning of life: Life as a journey or school vs. Life as art, life for the sake of living. While it is not my purpose here to sell either viewpoint, it's interesting to look at the ramifications of each.

Life as a Journey

There can be a lot of variation among perceptions of life as a journey or school. Some people think that we are here to learn and grow, to fulfill some purpose of our own, as biological or spiritual beings (depending on your viewpoint of our nature), or to fulfill some purpose of a higher order: our species, life itself, the universe or God (again, depending on your viewpoint). In this Life as a School frame of reference, we ideally learn from everything as we go, from every experience, both good and bad.

We may see the purpose of living as passing on the knowledge we gain to others, especially the next generations, or pushing ahead the vast body of human knowledge and experience. If you believe that you will go on after this life in some way, then the gathering of knowledge for its own sake becomes a valuable enterprise. Some examples of life as a journey or school are:

- Getting a degree.
- Starting a company.
- Starting a romantic relationship (even more so, *maintaining* such a relationship over the years).
- Raising a child who makes it out in the world.
- Looking over your day before going to sleep at night to see what you observed or learned that day.

> **The view of life as a journey, when we are fully engaged in it, can give us drive, purpose, progress, excitement and fulfillment.**

Exercise 1-8:

List some life activities that fall within the idea of life as a journey or learning and/or evolution.

Life as Art

Now let's look at life as art. What would this mean? Not everyone believes that life is a place for us to learn, grow and progress. Some see it as simply meant to be experienced or created in the moment, as fully as possible. Life as art means living mindfully in the moment. People in this frame of reference feel that looking at life as something that we are to progress through and learn from takes away from full existence in the moment. Of course we do learn things, but maybe the point of life is not the accumulation of skill or knowledge (after all, there will always be more that we don't yet know), but is about being here, now.

Life as art includes taking pleasure in daily activities. Enjoying cleaning the house, preparing a meal, driving to work, hearing from your family members how their days have gone are examples of life as art. The more present and mindful the activity, the more artful it is.

> **Life as art ideally means living creatively in the moment, as a fully present, fully expressed, fully experiencing creative act.**

You can increase the value of life by:

- Arranging your possessions in a way that pleases you.

- Making a meal that is attractive and tasty rather than just filling.

- Driving mindfully, noticing your surroundings.

- Listening to your family with real care and attention.

- Noticing your emotions without resisting them.

- Looking over your day before going to sleep at night to savor your experiences of that day.

Our abilities fluctuate as we move through life. Children have the ability to experience things with wonder, things that adults tend to see with jaded eyes. My husband and his friend took a walk at lunch time on a beautiful day. They stopped at a bookstore where his friend bought a new, expensive computer book that he had wanted to get. As they were walking back to work, they encountered a little boy saying ecstatically to his mother, "Look Mom, *a ladybug!*" My husband's friend said, "Darn! I know I'm never going to get as much enjoyment out of this book as that kid just got from a bug!"

Young people have the capacity for dreams and passion and excellence in physical pursuits such as sports that are sometimes dulled in older people. Adults have mastered many skills and have the freedom to apply what they have learned while seeking more skill and knowledge as they go. Retired people have the opportunity to relax and enjoy life and leisure pursuits, if they have planned well for this time in their lives and remain healthy. Very old people sometimes, while apparently losing abilities they once had, return to something like childlike wonder. If we consider life as art, each stage in life can be seen as something to be enjoyed for itself.

Exercise 1-9:

List some activities that illustrate life as art, or life for the sake of living.

Now, instead of trying to decide between these two world views let's try for integration of the two. Why not have life as a journey and life for the sake of living at the same time? If you have a clear preference for one of these views over the other, fine. If you want them both however, go for it.

Exercise 1-10:

- **Write, talk or think about your favorite of the above options: life as a journey, life for the sake of living, or an integration of the two.**
- **Why do you like it?**
- **How does it work for you in terms of understanding your own life? The lives of others?**
- **What about this world view do you find exciting or inspiring?**
- **If you liked the idea of integrating the two approaches, think about how you would do this.**

How do We Achieve and Maintain Our Potential?

Whatever works! You have strategies and methods that work for you or you wouldn't have made it this far in life. I believe the main thing is to take on life, to *live it*, rather than letting it just happen to us. If we live mindfully and with intention, pausing sometimes to look back to see how far we've come and to look forward to see if we are headed in the direction we want to go, if we make use of our abilities and explore our potential, then we can say that we have lived life to the fullest. One of the keys is the observation of what is working.

Two writing exercises

Exercise 1-11. Taking a look at an area of life that is difficult in some way or that you would like to improve. Examples:

- A relationship (parent, child, friend, life partner, boss, employee, pet, or neighbor for example)
- Your job, career, or business
- Your health, body image, or sense of well-being
- Your finances
- The condition of your possessions or your living space

Choose an area of life, either from the examples above or another that you are interested in. Write what you would call this area of life across the top of a blank piece of paper. Now draw a line vertically down the middle of the page under that. At the top of the first column write, "What has worked." At the top of the second column write, "What hasn't worked." See Fig. 1-1 on the following page for an example of what I mean.

Write, in any order they occur to you, the things that fit into these two categories. The two columns do not need to match in length. There is no wrong way to do this. If you are doing this in a group or with a partner, once you each feel done with your lists, share whatever you would like to with your partner about the lists themselves and observations you have come to while writing them.

Regarding My Job	
What Has Worked	*What Hasn't Worked*
A positive attitude.	A negative attitude.
Returning phone calls promptly.	Complaining about management (fun, but hasn't changed anything!)
Being willing to take on more responsibility.	Looking at this job as a 'stepping stone' to something better
Treating customers with respect.	:
:	.
.	

Worked/Hasn't Worked sample worksheet (Fig. 1-1)

This exercise can lead to quite comical revelations at times:

- One person realized that failing to return calls from prospective customers was hurting his business.

- Another realized that her filing system, which seemed crazy to others, actually worked just fine for her.

- Another man realized that color-coding his files was very helpful to him and that when he didn't do this he quickly lost track of things.

- A mother had followed the advice of others to be strict and stern with a cranky child. This exercise showed her that actually, calm patience worked better.

The process of writing down and then looking at what has worked and what hasn't worked allows us to see things that we already know at some level but have lost sight of.

Exercise 1-12:

Divide a page into two columns by drawing a vertical line down the middle. At the top of the first column write, "What I want in my life." At the top of the second write, "What I don't want in my life." Write things as they occur to you. As in the exercise above, the two columns do not have to match in length, and there is no wrong way to do this.

What I Want in My Life.	What I Don't Want in My Life.
Harmony.	Yelling.
Friends I can really talk to.	Frustration.
Satisfying work.	Negativity.
Living in the country.	Living in the city.
Flowers, music, good food.	A messy house.
Personal growth.	Stagnation.
⋮	⋮

Want/Don't Want sample worksheet (Fig. 1-2)

Some people are going to put down that they want peace and harmony in the household with no yelling and screaming. Others will say that they want a family situation where people tell the truth and work things out between them no matter what it takes, instead of pretending that everything is fine when it isn't. Neither is wrong, because this is person-centered work. Your own viewpoint is what counts for you. As a side effect of this exercise, examining what we want and do not want in life helps us to see whether we are likely to get what we want with our current strategies.

There is a wonderful Turkish saying (for which I am indebted to Jerry Davis), "No matter how far you've gone down the wrong road, turn back." Another way of looking at the same thing is, "If you keep going in the same direction, then you're going to end up where you're headed." A man who wants an attractive, cozy home, but who has the habit of throwing things anywhere and leaving them in disordered piles, may realize that there is some incongruence in his life. A woman who wants a close, loving family but who either consistently chooses men who abuse her, or who cannot seem to refrain from constantly criticizing her nearest and dearest, is unlikely to get what she wants that way. Quoting Robert Rich , again: "if something works, do more of it. If it doesn't work, try something else."

If you are doing this exercise in a group or with a partner, when you each feel done with your lists of what you want and do not want, share what you have written and observed with your partner. This exercise can really move some things around.

I taught a home-making/life skills class in a high school for several years. Partly to see if I was getting them to really think about life choices and partly just for their own benefit, I had them do Exercise 1-12 at the start and the end of the term. I collected up the papers from the first time and stored them. In this class, we talked about relationships, life styles, managing one's finances and one's possessions, responsibility for pets and children, meal planning and the impact good food has upon quality of life, and many, many other things. At the end of the term I had them do the writing exercise again and then compare what they had written with the first papers. It was fun to see how their thinking had expanded, from fairly materialistic and mostly just personal wants. The second set of lists often included more about the quality of relationships and about well-being in other areas of life than just the personal.

This is something you can do on your own by writing out the lists and seeing what you learn from doing that, then putting the paper away for six months or a year, doing it again and getting out the first paper to compare them. This is especially interesting to do if you are actively involved in some kind of personal growth work in the meantime.

Chapter Summary

When we look at how good life could potentially be we may be inspired (or possibly somewhat depressed), by the amount of room there is for improvement.

This book provides models and tools for improving daily life toward a theoretical ideal. There are always ups and downs in life, but we are aiming here at a condition of "much more up than down."

Two skills aid us in achieving happiness and fulfillment: The ability to have and appreciate what is, and the ability to change our surroundings to better suit our needs and wants.

The person-centered viewpoint aids our work toward a better quality of life. If the exercises in this book are done in that context they will yield much better results. Granting others their own viewpoints, their own points-from-which-to-view (which is to say their own beingness), makes room for a better quality of relationship.

We can look at life as a journey or school, where we are progressively accumulating knowledge and experience, or we can look at life as art, life for the sake of living. Either worldview gives us ways in which to maximize our enjoyment of life. If we choose to, we can integrate the two, taking the best from both.

How do we achieve and maintain our potential? Some answers to these questions are the focus of this book. The exercises offer practical ways to apply the material and make it your own.

2 Traumatic Stress as a Factor in Life

- The Effects of Traumatic Stress
- What Can be Done about these Effects?
- Triggering of Traumatic Incidents
- What is Resolution of Trauma?
- Attempted Solutions
- To Face It or Not to Face It?
- Real Resolution of Traumatic Stress
- Emotional First Aid: Three Simple Remedies

The Effects of Traumatic Stress

In the ground-breaking book *On Aggression*, Lorenz (1974) talked about his pet goose who followed him everywhere, as much as possible. The goose's devotion allowed Lorenz the opportunity to observe its behavior closely. The goose suffered a shock one day and on subsequent days Lorenz observed the goose to make a wide circle around the area where the traumatic experience had occurred, even though there was nothing there now to cause alarm. Over time, with no further shocks occurring in that location, the width of the circle the goose made to avoid that spot diminished, but the avoidance never completely went away.

On the biological level, it makes sense that organisms store up memories of danger or fear in order to avoid pain, injury or death in the future. It may be lowering to compare oneself to a goose, but human beings store traumatic memories with as much tenacity as geese do, with a resultant avoidance of certain places, people or situations. When we avoid a location or situation with no inherent danger in it, we limit our awareness, perception and options. In fact, we do so more than the goose, because our dangers include symbolic and social ones, not only physical events and places.

When an animal is injured the first thing it will do, if it possibly can, is scramble to its feet. Despite the fact that doing so will probably cause further pain, the instinct to get up drives the animal. The alternative, taking no action to get up, invites predators to come in to kill and eat the defenseless one. Emotionally, we do the same thing. Often a person who has just suffered an injury or a devastating shock or loss will answer, "Fine" when asked, "How are you doing?" Just labeling this as denial misses the deeper truth. The organism, animal or human, is trying not only to *look* fine in order to avoid attack, but trying to *be* fine.

There are two sides to that coin. We are taught as we grow up to pull ourselves together and refrain from wallowing in our hurts, but there is a strong biological imperative as well, to both *act as if* we are in control and to *be* in control of ourselves and (as far as is possible) our environment. The negative side to this is that we "stuff" things, storing up hurt, resistance, emotion and confusion in hard lumps that we then carry around with us. On the positive side, there is such a thing as resilience. We do have the ability to rise above our hurts and carry on. We will find ways to cope with whatever happens to us. Even if some of those coping mechanisms end up causing further problems, we're better off to acknowledge them as efforts to cope rather than condemn them as senseless activities.

In an ideal world, each person who suffered a trauma would hold it together as best as possible, coping with whatever had come up. Later, there would be a safe time and space to "unstuff" everything that happened including all the thoughts, intentions and feelings, as well as what actually happened. Usually in a traumatic event, too much happens too fast for us to be able to track with it. This very inability to receive and process all of the data coming in has a lowering effect upon awareness. Additionally, we have a tendency to depress our own consciousness when we anticipate that something unpleasant is about to happen, in an effort to avoid experiencing it.

The trouble is that attempting to put traumatic experience out of mind doesn't get rid of it. Storing painful memories takes some effort. Trying to keep a lid on them takes more effort. Conflicting with the intention and desire to keep these memories squashed down out of sight, we also have the desire to return to an ideal state of alertness, balance and comfort, which requires resolution.

> No matter how good we are at repressing painful memories, they continue to resurface: in dreams, in irrational thoughts and behaviors, in outbursts of emotion and in physical illness. They continue to demand attention and resolution.

Much has been made of a study[1] (Shalev & Yehuda, 1999) that showed that 53% of people in the study with Post-Traumatic Stress Disorder (PTSD), recovered without outside help within three months. While this is a good testimonial for human resilience, it misses the point that not all people who have experienced a traumatic event develop PTSD. Whether a person qualifies for a diagnosis of PTSD or not, she or he may still have residual effects from traumatic incidents that impact quality of life. PTSD can be a useful diagnosis. It identifies a cluster of symptoms, helps both sufferers and clinicians understand what is going on with the case, and helps researchers to study the phenomenon[2]. Much research has been done specifically on people who qualify for this diagnosis (which has also become a crucial point in qualifying for insurance coverage). Large segments of the population are affected by traumatic stress but are a symptom or two short of a full PTSD diagnosis. They tend to be neglected certainly in current academic studies, and even in treatment.

---

[1] Yehuda R, & Shalev A. (1998) "Predicting the development of posttraumatic stress disorder from the acute response to a traumatic event." *Biological Psychiatry* 44(12): 1305-13.

[2] See the American Psychiatric Association's *Diagnostic and Statistical Manual of Mental Disorders, Fourth Edition*, 2000.

What Can be Done about the Effects of Traumatic Incidents?

Traumatic Incident Reduction (TIR, part of the larger subject of Metapsychology), is the most effective and efficient method of resolving the effects of traumatic incidents, according to my observation. (See the Appendix B, especially: www.tir.org for more information, also the book *Beyond Trauma: Conversations on Traumatic Incident Reduction, 2nd Ed.* (V. Volkman, 2005), which you can preview at www.BeyondTrauma.com).

While this Life Skills book doesn't give you the training to do TIR, the theory behind it is very useful in daily life. Of course there are many things besides traumatic incidents that have a significant effect on our ability to function well in life, such as worries, upsets, confusions, misunderstandings and regretted actions to mention a few. Still, past traumatic incidents, large and small, cause some of the most significant impact on the quality of our lives. Understanding this impact allows us to understand emotions and behaviors in ourselves and others that were previously inexplicable.

Interestingly enough, modern film and fiction are getting more and more psychologically sophisticated and accurate in relation to the effects of stored trauma and the phenomenon of *triggering*, which we address in the next section. Of course there are still plenty of inaccurate representations as well, but the general improvement makes for much more interesting and satisfying entertainment.

Let's look a little further at resilience, a subject of great interest because it affects our ability to bounce back from difficult experiences and to live well. Resilience is so intuitively important to our survival that there are more individuals and organizations currently studying the subject than ever before, judging by a quick survey of the Internet.

Someone once asked me the difference between resilience and a prideful, hard heart. Pride and a hard heart are defense mechanisms a person uses to try to protect self from distressing experiences. Unfortunately they have the byproduct of making him/her more rigid and inflexible, and hence less able to respond to the environment intelligently and adroitly. Resilience, on the other hand is either the physical property of being able to bounce back into its former shape when compressed (as in, "Foam rubber is resilient.") or the emotional ability to return to a good state rather quickly after something bad happens. Resilience in the second meaning means a person who is strong without being brittle. S/he has inner resources, and the ability to inspire and utilize support from those around him/her in order to return to a steady state.

A prideful, hard-hearted person definitely comes across to others as callous. A resilient person is more relaxed, less defensive, more comfortable in his/her own skin, so to speak, so he responds to others more readily and appropriately. The former is afraid of being hurt. The latter knows that if hurt, s/he will recover, so s/he is more willing to invest in relationships. Someone with less resilience stays "dented" longer—maybe permanently.

To what degree can resilience be inherited? Affected by environmental factors? Deliberately enhanced? These are the questions being asked. The good news is that resilient behaviors and strategies (see Goleman, *Emotional Intelligence*, 1997) can be learned and practiced. Also, resolving a trauma does more than improve a person's resilience by releasing the stored up pain and resistance. The actual work of facing up to and mastering a previously overwhelming experience strengthens the person's confidence and resilience.

Triggering of Traumatic Incidents

Understanding the concept of triggering or *restimulation*:

1. Can help one to understand one's own (less than perfectly sane) behavior and that of others.
2. Can help one to avoid needless restimulation of self and others (examples: scary movies, trigger phrases, geographic locations, etc.).

Triggering occurs when an incident from the past is brought alive again, restimulated, by something that happens in the present. The current event brings up the past incident. A person getting triggered may or may not have a conscious awareness of the restimulated past experience. In any case, there is something repressed and not fully remembered for a triggered incident from the past to have an effect on the person's current feelings or behavior.

A man might say, "I hate funerals. They always make me feel so bad." We might assume that, because he has a conscious memory of all the funerals he has attended, that this bad feeling comes up as the sum total of his sad experiences at these funerals. In fact though, there is something un-remembered or un-viewed about these incidents for this cumulative feeling to arise every time he has to go to another funeral. Another factor may be at work as well. There may be an earlier loss, an earlier incident that is similar in some respect (usually in the strong feeling it contains) that is not consciously remembered at all but that is nevertheless triggered along with all of these funeral experiences. That earlier unseen incident will anchor the bad feelings of the later ones until it is resolved.

A woman might say, "I just can't stand men with red hair," without having any rational explanation for her feelings. One of the uses of TIR is to follow down a specific feeling to its root, even if that is an incident of which the client/viewer has no conscious memory. Strong negative feelings toward something, even things that most people will agree that they don't like, will be found to have deeper roots than present experience alone.

Even though there is a lot to understand about the subject, just knowing that restimulation can and does happen frequently in life can increase our understanding of ourselves and others.

Exercise 2-1:

- **Remember a time when you observed someone reacting to something in what seemed to be an overblown or inappropriate manner.**
- **Consider the fact that there was almost certainly something that got triggered for that person to have reacted in that way.**
- **Observe whether understanding the concept of triggering has any effect on your feelings about what happened.**
- **Remember some similar times as above for as long as you are interested or until you get a positive shift.**

Note: Restimulation is no excuse for seriously anti-social behavior. It is the job of every human being to learn to control his or her actions, despite the provocation of restimulation. This is what it means to be civilized. This is what it means to be grown up.

Exercise 2-2:

Remember some times when you found yourself feeling or acting in an irrational way. Were you aware of the irrationality at the time, or did you only become aware of it later? Observe whether an understanding of the phenomenon of triggering has any effect on your feelings of that event.

Beyond helping us to understand and be more compassionate toward ourselves and others, a working knowledge of restimulation can help us to avoid it to some extent. We do not want to use this to avoid life. Something getting triggered is a signal to us that there is something we may need to work on. Meanwhile we can be aware of what is happening. Resilience to restimulation grows with the successful mental/emotional work one does. Resilience is increased by both inward-looking, therapeutic types of work (when they successfully resolve past traumas) and types of training that give a person more command over his/her mental and emotional world.

In terms of consciously avoiding triggers, some things make more sense to avoid, for instance, scary movies. If they upset you and leave you feeling less aware and less happy, just don't go to see them. You won't be missing out on a big aspect of life by avoiding scary movies. You protect and take care of yourself when you consciously make a choice to avoid being triggered. Watching or reading the "news" can be put in this category as well.

If you strongly dislike paying your bills though, and get upset and restimulated when you do it, avoidance will be unlikely to produce a positive outcome. You can be aware of the restimulation and acknowledge that it is there, which will usually help somewhat, if only to help you take the whole thing less seriously. Then you could go on to choose to take some positive action to resolve the causes of this triggering which may include some new life strategies to bring your finances to a better state.

> When we become aware of our own behavior, especially our own less-than-perfectly-rational behavior, we have greater understanding and more personal power to act in saner and more creative ways.

All too often, we seek to get rid of people or things that trigger us, rather than getting to the bottom of what is being triggered. Once the old baggage is cleared up completely, there is nothing left to become restimulated. At that point, a person or situation that used to upset us will no longer do so. In a situation (short of physical or verbal abuse) when you tend to get triggered despite a lack of any current danger, the best thing to do is to notice the *fact* of the restimulation and not take it too seriously. Being aware of it is half the battle.

If you feel, "Every time I go to my mother-in-law's house, I get upset," the consequences of avoidance in this case may include hurting your spouse and causing discord in the family. In a situation where you will end up causing yourself or others more pain by avoiding something, you can take some action to get rid of the source of distress rather than getting rid of the trigger itself. Instead of continuing to be the effect of uncomfortable situations, you can do something effective to improve things. Many of the exercises in this book can be used to gain more resilience.

Exercise 2-3:
- **List situations or things that trigger you.**
- **Separate them into the things you can reasonably avoid and the things you need to be able to face up to.**
- **Look at what strategies you have tried for times when you get triggered. Which ones worked? Which did not?**

Being aware of the whole concept of triggering and how it happens also allows us greater understanding of others. If someone is restimulated and as a consequence of that, acting irrationally, trying to talk them out of it is often worse than useless. Getting someone to tell you exactly how he or she feels and letting him or her know that you really heard and understood is often the most effective method. (Also see the book, *Non-Violent Communication*, Rosenberg, 1999.)

Exercise 2-4:

- Remember a time when someone you had to deal with (either in your family or at work) was acting in an especially irrational way.
- What did you do?
- How did that work?
- What else might you have tried?
- Remember as many of these as you wish to.

Children, for some reason, are experts at observing what triggers their parents, their siblings, and their friends, and are often ruthless in the application of this knowledge. To be fair, it is tough to be a child sometimes. One has so little control over one's environment. It may seem in that circumstance that all is fair in terms of getting one's own way. Hopefully as adults we have out-grown the almost irresistible urge to tease and trigger our nearest and dearest.

Of course we can easily restimulate another without the least intention to do so. Living closely with others though can teach us certain things that can be pretty well guaranteed to set them off.

Exercise 2-5:
- Think of someone you care for and know well.
- Make a list of situations or statements that tend to trigger this person.
- Consider how you might use this awareness to make life more pleasant for you and for that other person.
- Repeat as long as you are interested or until you get a positive shift.

If you wish to avoid needlessly restimulating people, one fairly easy change to make is to avoid the use of "You…" statements. You know the ones: "You look tired," "You look terrible," "You need to [do X, Y and Z about your life]", "You are [stupid, wrong, insensitive, fill in the blank]." Or just, "You should…" Really, any of these sorts of statements is unlikely to produce a harmonious result. It is always better to ask than to tell, if you are talking to another person about themselves.

Now let's move on from avoidance as a strategy to looking at full resolution of the effects of traumatic stress.

What is Resolution of Trauma?

Human beings have been pursuing effective ways of dealing with the effects of trauma as long as there have been human beings.

How do we know when full resolution of a past event is attained?

1. There is no more triggering of the past event. This includes no more flashbacks (behaving or feeling as if the event were actually happening all over again). The memory of the event still exists, but the emotion burden has been discharged.

2. A person experiences comfort and ease in circumstances where there was stress and pain before.

3. Often at the point of resolution, which we call an *end point*, some sort of re-alization occurs. It can be anything from small to profound, e.g. anything from the awareness that a situation doesn't bother one any more, to a reali-zation that may have a significant positive impact on one's life.

The knowledge that real resolution is possible is therapeutic in itself.

The belief commonly gets expressed that once something awful has happened to you, you are "scarred for life." While this may be true in the sense of a physical scar, complete resolution of mental and physical trauma is possible in most cases. In the situation of a complex trauma, it may need to be compartmentalized and addressed one piece at a time for full resolution. Once a particular incident, part of an incident, or aspect of a situation is handled fully, it will no longer be triggered again as traumatic material.

Attempted Solutions to the Effects of Traumatic Stress

Human beings have been pursuing effective ways of dealing with the effects of trauma as long as there have been human beings. Some methods have been more life-affirming than others. Not so long ago, people suffering from traumatic stress were told to forget the incidents that caused it. Left with that option as the only help they were given, they turned to other things in pursuit of peace and happiness. Here is a list of some common strategies:

- Anesthetization via alcohol, though legal, socially acceptable and widely popular, can cause new problems on top of the old (anesthetized but not resolved) problems.

- Drugs, either prescription, or street drugs, can do the same.

- Addictive behaviors such as compulsive gambling, sexual activities, computer addiction, being a workaholic, etc., ditto.

- Another common solution to the tormenting effects of past traumatic incidents, rather the opposite of all the avoidance techniques listed above, is deliberately putting oneself in harm's way, either through dangerous sports, hobbies, or careers. Of course not all athletes or skydivers or firefighters are necessarily acting out of an attempt to anesthetize past experience. The way to tell the difference between someone who is and someone who isn't is to look at whether the activity has a quality of being *driven*, as distinct from a natural enthusiasm for an activity or career the person enjoys.

- Another is compulsive over-achievement.

A firefighter driven by traumatic incidents who does the work to resolve those past traumas, will not necessarily quit being a firefighter, but will be a more present, effective firefighter, who will take more pleasure in the job.

> It is a fact that we act out of past experiences. We all do it.
> To the degree we do it unconsciously, we are less resilient, less present, less causative in our lives.

To Face it or Not to Face it?

Certainly there are times when we cannot face up to past traumas:

- When we have not had enough food or sleep or are in acute pain.
- When life problems press in too hard on us, demanding immediate attention.
- When we are already triggered into too much negative experience (what we sometimes call "over-restimulated").

These are not the times to delve into past traumatic events. When in good condition to do the work, and using an effective technique, clients often remark that is was actually easier to face the experiences that haunted them than it was to carry around the effects of those experiences and try not to look at them.

Modern film and fiction are getting generally better at accurately showing not only the effects of trauma and triggering, but also the positive results than can be obtained by facing past traumas.

Exercise 2-6:

Think of some books, movies, plays or television shows that you think have done a poor job of accurately depicting:
- The effects of traumatic stress.
- The effects of facing up to past traumas.

Think of some books, movies, plays or television shows that you think have done a good job of accurately depicting:
- The effects of traumatic stress.
- The effects of facing up to past traumas.

Real Resolution of Traumatic Experience

Although I am talking about the method of Traumatic Incident Reduction (TIR) which I have found most useful for dealing permanently with the effects of traumatic stress, I am not saying that this method is the only one that can be effective. There are many things that work to a greater or lesser degree.

First is the option of human beings working through trauma on their own without any outside help. It can be done and can be very effective. It tends to take a long time, much ability, and may require more resilience than most people have. Remember that we are not talking about just "feeling better" about the memory of the traumatic event, but full resolution as defined above. Some people think that anything else than doing it on your own is cheating.

> There is a crucial difference between an emotionally charged past event dropping out of restimulation without full resolution, and that same thing being completely resolved, never to come up as an issue again.

The saying that, "Time heals all wounds" is not quite true. What the passage of time can do, especially if one is not suffering any further shocks during that period, is to allow the traumatic incident to drop out of restimulation, until another trigger comes along. Many factors affect our ability to throw off the effects of traumatic stress: health and nutrition issues, success or lack thereof in the work place, the state of our important relationships, and major world events, to name some of the obvious ones.

As covered earlier in this chapter, traumatic stress does not equal Post-Traumatic Stress Disorder, nor the reverse. PTSD-diagnosed people tend to be in a constant or frequent state of restimulation as well as being highly susceptible to further restimulation from random events (low resilience). Though the majority of us would not qualify for a diagnosis of PTSD, the "normal" human condition is to carry some amount of restimulated material around most of the time. In fact we are so good at this, so strong we might even say, that this seems OK to us.

Two forces are at work throughout a person's life: the downward drag of accumulated trauma, modified by the chronic and acute levels of restimulation, vs. the person's drive toward life. That drive consists of the built-in biological imperative all living things have to pursue and maintain survival, plus the individual's inborn and learned resilience. These forces manifest as the urge to bounce back, fight back, to learn from experience, and to work toward greater survival for oneself and relations.

Exposure techniques (which involve having a person contact traumatic events and re-experience them, either in a group or individual setting) are other ways to attempt resolution of past traumas. Some can be quite rough. (For further information on such things I refer you to *Beyond Trauma: Conversations on Traumatic Incident Reduction*, 2nd *Ed.*, V. Volkman, 2005, especially Dr. Robert Moore's article on the value of exposure and also the chapter on veterans' experiences with different types of exposure therapies.)

Many studies show exposure therapies to be effective. From the philosophical point of view of Applied Metapsychology, a safe, person-centered setting is essential for optimum results. Exposure therapy done in unsafe settings has given that method a bad name in some quarters. Re-traumatization can occur if a person is put back into a traumatic event and left with restimulated material stirred up but not resolved. Part of the safety factor of TIR is that each area taken up is thoroughly addressed to a point of resolution and each session is taken to an end point. Enthusiastic practitioners of TIR find it efficient, thorough and effective.

Dr. Gerbode notes that effective trauma resolution produces considerable benefits in terms of personal growth ("Applied Metapsychology: Therapy or Personal Growth", 1995), beyond the mere fact of relief from painful memories.

There is a saying, "Whatever doesn't kill you makes you stronger." That is true if you have the opportunity to process the material fully and learn what can be learned from it. It's not true if you are carrying a residue of pain, resistance, and lowered awareness around in the form of unresolved traumatic incidents.

Emotional First Aid – Three Simple Remedies

Now, what to do if you find yourself restimulated and without a handy TIR practitioner? (See www.tir.org for a list of practitioners and for information on training.) There are some simple Remedies that you can do on your own or working with another person. A *Remedy*, as I use the word here, is a relatively brief technique used to destimulate a person. It is emotional first-aid.

Once you are in a calmer frame of mind, the exercises and information in the rest of the book may be useful to you as well. Three simple Remedies follow. There are more Remedies in Chapter Seven, but these three may be best for acute restimulation.

Each of these Remedies can be done any number of times.

The Large Object Remedy

- Find a large, unmoving object, or a large body of water, or a large tree.
- Sit facing it, and just notice it, look at it, until you feel calmer and more stable, or brighter.

How large is large? You can use a building, though most people prefer an object in nature: a lake or ocean, a large rock, a hill, or even a mountain. Choose any large object that appeals to you for this exercise.

This is best done outdoors, but can even work with a bedridden person, using something they can see out of the window, or the largest possible object in a room, such as a whole wall. Don't force it, especially with a person who is ill. With a sick or otherwise fragile person, several shorter periods will probably work better than one long one. The value of this technique comes from a person contacting the physical world in the present moment.

Take a Walk

Of course, the benefits of walking for both physical health and mental well-being are well known. This Remedy involves not only walking, but deliberately noticing objects as you go until you feel brighter and more present. Anyone can do this alone. For a person who is feeling overwhelmed or shaky, it is more beneficial to have another person go along and point out things to notice. This might sound too simplistic to be of use, but is surprisingly effective and again, it is not meant to be an entire solution to a difficult situation.

Exercise 2-7:

Try "Take A Walk" by yourself and with others and notice what results you get. A short, deliberate period of noticing things in one's environment on a daily basis can help to raise awareness and presence.

Stephen Covey, in his well-known, highly recommended book, *The Seven Habits of Highly Effective People* (1990), provides a useful model for paying attention to how we can use our energy to best effect. In his model, there is a large circle labeled "Circle of Concern" and a smaller one within it labeled "Circle of Influence". There may be many things of which we are aware that we cannot directly influence. For instance, if you are distressed about the burning of rain forests in South America, there is not much you can directly do to affect that, short of taking a trip to see what could be done. If you chose that course of action there would naturally be a tradeoff. To go there you would have to leave behind all of your responsibilities at home.

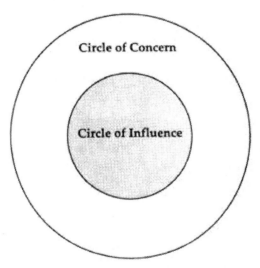

Covey's Circles of Influence & Concern (Fig. 2-1)

Covey recommends putting your attention on the things within your own circle of influence, those things you can actually do something to affect. If we do this, he says, our circle of influence tends to grow larger. If we put our attention in our circle of concern, outside of our circle of influence, we feel less and less able to affect the things about which we are concerned. Because of the Information Age we are living in, human beings now have the ability to be aware of more things going on around the world that need care and attention than we have ever been able to know about before. Depressing, isn't it?

This probably has as much to do with the rate of depression in the population today as anything else. Watching the news amounts to having someone tell you, "Look at all of these awful things that you can't do anything about." It's enough to depress anyone. Often there is something you can do: vote, recycle, pick up the litter someone else has dropped, send a donation, buy from companies that take real care of the environment. Of course these things can and do make a difference. You might not be able to help the child you see in the news, but you can be kind to the children you do encounter.

Exercise 2-8:

Draw or list the subjects and issues that belong in your own Circle of Influence and Circle of Concern. For some period of time, do the best you can to focus your attention in your Circle of Influence. Notice what results you get in how you feel and in your energy level.

Can-Do Remedy

You can write this, think it, or do it with another person. Choose an area of trouble or worry in your life. Considering that area, ask yourself: *"In this area, what can I really do?"*

Notice and acknowledge (or have your partner acknowledge) each separate answer as you go, answering the question over and over until you get to a positive shift.

We are looking for positive answers here, but they can be very small ones, such as: "Wash the dishes", "Tie my shoes", "Say 'Good morning,' to my boss tomorrow". Do these until you feel brighter or something shifts in a positive direction for you.

If you can't find anything you can do within the area in question, then broaden your search to look for things you can definitely do that improve anything at all to some degree. My mother was a great advocate of housework as therapy. No matter how bad things get you can usually do something around the house to make it cleaner or neater. The fact of doing something that gets a positive result gets one out of the "I can't do anything about anything" frame of mind.

Chapter Summary

Traumatic stress affects everyone at some point in life. This is obvious in the case of Post-Traumatic Stress Disorder, but every life contains some hurts and losses that can have a lingering effect.

Resilience plays an important role in how much a person is affected by traumatic events and for how long a period of time. Resilience can be strengthened by doing good work on trauma resolution.

Past traumatic events can become triggered when events with some similar content or feeling occur. This is part of our survival equipment as living creatures. A similar situation to a traumatic incident can stimulate a strong urge to fight or to run away, even if there is no danger present.

People have tried many sorts of solutions to the pain and discomfort of traumatic stress. Often those attempted solutions cause further difficulties.

Real resolution of traumatic stress is possible, with a person retaining the ability to remember and make use of any knowledge gained during traumatic events, but free of the pain, effort, charge and resistance s/he had been carrying around with those incidents.

3 Predicting and Understanding Emotion

- What is the Emotional Scale?
- Chronic, Acute and Projected Emotional Levels
- Cause or Effect? Using the Emotional Scale as Tool
- The Predictability Factor
- Using the Emotional Scale to Create Positive Effects

Tempting as it is to judge people, the point of the exercises in this chapter is not judgment of self or others, but increased understanding. If you find yourself slipping into judgment or criticism of yourself or others, try just acknowledging it and moving on.

What is the Emotional Scale?

Whole books could be written about the observed phenomena of the Emotional Scale. The Scale is simply a spectrum of emotions (see Fig. 3-1 on the following page). I am calling it a spectrum rather than just a list of emotions because the theory is that each of the emotions follows or flows into the next, whether one is on the way down, or on the way up the scale. They aren't sharply divided, but rather shade into each other as do the colors of the rainbow. Of course many other emotions could be identified on this spectrum. Figure 3-1 shows the main ones that we tend to work with and talk about all the time.

ELATION
ENTHUSIASM
CHEERFULNESS
CONSERVATISM
COMPLACENCY
CONTENTMENT
AMBIVALENCE
ANTAGONISM
ANGER
RESENTMENT
HIDDEN HOSTILITY
ANXIETY
FEAR
GRIEF
APATHY

The Emotional Scale (Fig. 3-1)

Exercise 3-1: After familiarizing yourself with the Emotional Scale, think of some emotions that are not named on the scale. Where would you put them?

First of all, let us clarify that there is nothing "wrong" with any of these emotions. They are all appropriate in different circumstances. Two of the things that are interesting to study in relation to emotions are:

1. Fixidity or stuckness of a person's emotional level.

2. The appropriateness or inappropriateness of a given emotion in a particular situation.

Of course, that last is a value judgment, and working in a person-centered way, we need to be mindful of that. The fact remains that anyone expressing an emotion that is truly inappropriate to the situation will also probably experience some discomfort along with it. It isn't true that just because an emotion is far down the scale that it is necessarily terribly unpleasant. If someone has done the work to clear out the traumatic aspects of past losses, for example, s/he may experience a new loss as a very pure and in-the-present-moment Grief. This is a very different experience from feeling a loss all muddied up with the left-over feelings of sadness from earlier losses.

Any emotion can have an aesthetic component to it. We can enjoy the beautiful sadness at a tear-jerker movie, or enjoy a delicious thrill of fear in a haunted house. The situations in these examples may be artificial, but the emotions are real.

Another way to look at and understand the Emotional Scale is to consider it as a range of vibration from heavy and slow at the bottom to light and fast at the top. Let's take a look at each of the major emotional levels from the bottom to the top.

Apathy contains a sense of hopelessness, as if the effort to "do something about it" (whatever "it" is), is just too great to contemplate. It is clearly not a very fun emotion, either to be in or to be around, but it can sometimes come with a sort of comfortable numbness, relative to some of the more volatile emotions above it on the scale.

At least a period of temporary Apathy might be expected after a stunning loss such as one's house and possessions being lost in a fire or other disaster; the loss of a business one had poured one's life into; or the loss of a long-term life partner. Some of the main factors determining how long that period of Apathy would last are: the person's own resilience, the support system available, and how much earlier traumatic material got restimulated.

Grief covers the gamut from acute frantic despair down to dull sadness, and everything in between. The emotional level of Grief is often accompanied by crying, but a person doesn't have to be crying to be at this level. As a side note, my sister Ellen points out that getting a cold often happens right after a loss of some kind and, "a cold is a slow way of crying." Psycho-neuroimmunology informs us that depression and lower emotions drag the immune system down.

After some period of Apathy in the examples given above, a person may move up into Grief. Again, depending on the circumstances, a person may move through Grief relatively quickly or stay parked there for years. Both Apathy and Grief are heavy, gluey emotions. In this band, a person tends to have most of his/her attention focused inward.

At <u>Fear,</u> a person is starting to look more outward, if only to watch for things that are—or appear to be—sources of threat or danger. Fear may manifest in a person's gaze tending to be frozen, the deer in the headlights phenomenon, or the gaze darting around, scanning the environment for danger.

Though it is up from Apathy and Grief and more active than those lower emotions, Fear is still not a very comfortable place to reside. Extreme fear is one of the worst emotions to experience. Fear spans the range from griefy, overwhelmed Fear up through a more prickly and outward-facing Fear. Any emotion can vary in volume or intensity as well as the emotional level itself. Fear can vary in intensity from stark terror through a low simmering anxiety.

<u>Hidden Hostility</u> comes between Fear and Anger. The Fear still has enough of a grip that hostility doesn't come out into the open as such, but is veiled. At the same time the person's reach is extending outward more now. Hidden Hostility shows when someone smiles at you while saying something that cuts you to the heart. Especially if this is a repeating pattern, the communication is coming from a place of Hidden Hostility.

Everyone hurts others inadvertently at times. Someone at the level of Hidden Hostility though, makes a habit of saying and doing hurtful things while pretending friendship or at the least, indifference. The psychological term for this is 'passive-aggressive behavior'.

At <u>Resentment,</u> hostility is now out in the open, though it is seething and simmering rather than lashing out. At this point, a person has moved up out of the long shadow of Apathy and is starting to feel that although the current situation is unfavorable, something might be (and should be!) done about it.

Not yet fully owning his or her personal power and responsibility, someone at Resentment is starting to cause bigger effects on the environment, though this person would prefer that the work be done by someone else.

<u>Anger</u> has the strongest outward focus so far. It comes in either hot or cold mode. This emotion can be a powerful force for getting things done; at the same time it can be very harsh and abrasive if directed either at self or other people. Anger can be a positive force if it is directed at appropriate situations and properly focused. It has a very bad name with many people I believe, because of its getting mixed up with another phenomenon. See Chapter Eight for a discussion of this.

<u>Antagonism</u> brings in a lighter note of playfulness for the first time as we move up the scale. Here a person is looking for change (usually in the object of his/her antagonism) but without the heaviness of Resentment. Since it is lighter, less serious, and more bantering, relationships based in Antagonism can look wildly successful compared to relationships between people much farther down the scale. Fiction, especially in TV and film, portray this sort of relationship often between the leading characters, whether they be couples, friends or people who work together. Trading witty quips, though not the pinnacle of intimacy, makes for lively entertainment and from some vantage points on the emotional scale may look to be as good as it gets.

At <u>Ambivalence,</u> a person has achieved a sort of autonomy. In fact in the whole band of Ambivalence – Contentment – Complacency we see a new tolerance for situations and other people. At Ambivalence, a person is still looking for something outside of him or her to come along and provide some interest and entertainment. This person has a very "take it or leave it" attitude toward life.

At <u>Contentment,</u> a person does not have a big drive to get things done, but is a master at enjoying what is. A person in Contentment is generally very pleasant to be around.

At <u>Complacency,</u> a person is more actively pleased in what s/he has wrought in the world. At Contentment and Complacency, a person has got life about where s/he wants it to be and interested in conserving and maintaining this achievement.

<u>Cheerfulness</u> a new plateau of engagement and activity, as a person at this level is very willing to reach out and involve others in his or her schemes.

Enthusiasm brings another level of intensity to the person's degree of causativeness. Where we saw a person at Ambivalence looking about (even if languidly) for something interesting to come along, at Cheerfulness and Enthusiasm s/he is looking around for new games to start. Explorers, inventors, and entrepreneurs are often (though certainly not always) in the cheerful-enthusiastic band.

Engagement and the Emotional Scale

The Emotional Scale shows a pattern of alternating greater and lesser engagement with the environment. Apathy is much disengaged due the loss of hope. Moving up, we get to the intensely engaged level of Anger. In Ambivalence through Complacency we see another sort of lesser engagement. Higher up we get intense engagement again at the level of Enthusiasm. The theoretical top of the scale would be bliss or serenity, another band of disengagement. We will look more at the issue of engagement in the Chapter Six (Success).

A person at Apathy and one at Ambivalence may both say that they are "bored", but there is an entirely different character to the experience of boredom at these two levels.

Exercise 3-2:

Think of one or more characters from fiction, film or TV that are good examples of each one of these emotional levels.

Exercise 3-3:

Since the scale represents a real set of phenomena, we find fictional characters who realistically move up and down this scale to be satisfying. In poorly written fiction, the characters may jump around from one level to another for no apparent reason.

- Think for some examples of fictional characters that you especially liked. Think about how they moved on the emotional scale and why.

- Think of some work of fiction (written, film, drama) that you didn't like or found annoying. Was there something unconvincing about the emotional levels of those characters, or how they changed from one emotion to another? What about that did not seem right to you?

While we are talking about emotions, let's talk about animals for a moment. (I am tempted to go off on a long tangent here, but will restrain myself. If this topic interests you, see my note to you in the Afterword.) There is quite a bit of emotional debate about whether animals have emotions or not. If it amuses you to do so, try the exercise 3-4.

Exercise 3-4:

- Observe an animal, whether a domesticated dog or cat, or a wild bird, or whatever.
- Can you observe the emotional level of this animal?
- As you watch it, do you notice any changes in its emotional level?
- What causes it to move either up or down the scale?

Chronic, Acute and Projected Emotional Levels

Emotions manifest in both acute and chronic forms. To use the Emotional Scale as a tool for understanding people, you need to be aware of this. A person chronically in the Ambivalent to Contentment band will experience acute Grief at the loss of a loved one, though this person is likely to come back up the scale relatively sooner and faster than someone who is chronically much lower on the scale. A person who lives chronically at the level of Grief may rise up to an acute, and possibly brief, state of Enthusiasm at winning a lottery or falling in love.

The acute/chronic question may seem complex enough. Besides this, s/he soon learns to project a pretended or "social" emotional level. The face shown to the world, if it doesn't harmonize with how s/he actually feels, is a projected emotional level, so that is another factor to be aware of.

We tend to be most comfortable with emotions at or close to our own chronic emotional band. Emotions much higher or lower than ours can seem unreal or annoying. Too much Grief or Apathy is hard to take after a while. Some people chronically in Fear project Anger as a more powerful-seeming place to come from. (Some people would say that this is true of all anger, that fear underlies it. I think that there are real differences in vibration and attitude at the two levels. Please do some observation for yourself and see what you think.) Hidden Hostility is by its very nature a projection of a pleasant emotion over the top of an unpleasant one. For people low on the scale, the vitality and energy of people at the top may be intolerable. Instead, they think, "Bah Humbug, nobody is really that happy."

Exercise 3-5:

1. **Recall a time when someone around you was dragging around in a very low emotional state when you were feeling pretty good. What was your response to the other person's emotion?**

2. **Recall a time when you were feeling relatively miserable emotionally and someone very cheerful was around (sincerely cheerful, not phony). What was your response to the other person's emotion?**

People inhabiting the high reaches of the Emotional Scale also may learn to mask their true feelings after being met with intolerance. This commonly happens to children when adults at lower emotional levels cannot face high volume Enthusiasm and squelch it.

> Mature people in the high bands of the scale can learn to communicate in a way that will be real to others at any emotional level without feeling any diminishment of their own level.

Here is a paradox: It is an ability to be able to control one's emotions so as to be professional, polite, and socially acceptable. Judith Martin (a.k.a. the famous Miss Manners) is a great proponent of civilization and looks with horror upon people who think that they should be "natural" all of the time or, even worse, bring up their children to believe that it is their right to be natural at all times. Too often "natural" in that context means out-of-control and obnoxious. On the other hand, people who are fully in their actual state of being without defense or pretense can have a powerful effect on their environments due to being fully present.

Exercise 3-6:

- **Think about (or discuss) the relative merits of projected, polite or social emotional levels compared to people being just where they chronically are.**
- **Are there situations where one mode of operation is more appropriate?**
- **Are there situations where the opposite is true?**

It is a vital skill for therapists and others in the helping professions to be able to recognize and face up to all of the human emotions.

Exercise 3-7:

1. Using lines of dialog from a book or magazine, practice with a partner portraying each of the emotions convincingly from the bottom of the scale to the top. Notice how it feels both to project and to receive each of these emotions. Does it make sense to you to think of each of these levels having a different (and lighter as you go up the scale) vibration or frequency?

2. With a partner, go to a busy place with lots of people and practice spotting the chronic emotional level of as many people as you can until you feel an increase in your awareness and ability to observe.

3. In life, observe instances of a people projecting a "social" emotional level on top of their actual chronic level. Are you able to identity the social level? The actual level? Spot as many of these as you can.

4. If you are willing, observe instances of yourself projecting a social emotional level on top of your actual level until you get a shift in awareness.

Cause or Effect? Using the Emotional Scale as a Tool

What is ideal in terms of emotion? It is the ability to move up and down easily and appropriately on the scale, and to experience the full range of the emotions. While it is possible to get stuck in the lower emotions, there is no such thing as being stuck at the top. Generally, the higher a person's chronic emotional level is, the more mobile s/he is on the scale. If someone appears to be fixed near the top of the scale, you can bet that is a false or projected emotion. Someone who "never gets mad" is chronically stuck below the level of Anger.

Every emotion, as mentioned before, has its own attractions. However, getting stuck somewhere isn't fun. Every time a person completes a good piece of personal work (whether within the context of Applied Metapsychology or any other subject) s/he not only moves up the Emotional Scale, but gains more mobility, even if just in relation to one area of life.

Another point to consider is the effect we have on each other. There is an emotional drag effect sort of like gravity or like the tides. If we spend time with people who are lower on the Emotional Scale than we are, unless we are very resilient, it's hard not to feel somewhat brought down. Similarly, if we are around someone who is up the scale from us, spending time with that person may tend to bring us up too. Another way to look at this is the concept of vibrational resonance. This phenomenon is always present. Some sensitive people are very easily influenced or pulled one way or the other, while others are more stable in themselves and resistant to influence.

You might decide all sorts of things based on this phenomenon. You might decide to only hang out with people at or near your own chronic emotional level for the sake of comfort and familiarity. There is a lot of this kind of self-sorting that people and groups go through and for that very reason. You might decide to avoid people who are low on the scale at all costs, though it could make life complex to follow that rule. You could decide to track down people who are high on the scale in order to benefit from their positions relative to your own.

Probably the best way to use this knowledge of the Emotional Scale is to practice getting more and more aware of it. The more aware you are of the emotional levels of yourself and others, the more understanding you will have. Understanding itself is enough often to move us from effect to cause. If you realize that someone in your environment chronically resides at Hidden Hostility, you will not be as likely to be surprised or hurt by this person's covertly attacking remarks.

There is a marvelous piece of work by Dr. Gerbode, called the Table of Attitudes (see Fig. 3-2 on following page), which plots out typical attitudes for each of the Emotional Scale levels across 20 different life factors. See Appendix B, to obtain this table. The Table of Attitudes does make recognition of and prediction of the various emotional bands much easier, besides having other uses.

The other way to use knowledge of the Emotional Scale is by paying attention to those things which tend to empower us to move stably upward on the scale.

ANTAGONISM	I don't like it.	You can't do it, and I can.	It's mine; you can't have it.
ANGER	I hate it.	I will make you unable to do it.	I'll destroy those who are trying to take things away from me.
RESENTMENT	It isn't fair.	They won't let me do it.	It's not fair that they should have things I don't.
HIDDEN HOSTILITY	I'll let them think everything's fine.	Able people are dangerous.	I'll have it, providing they don't realize what is happening.
ANXIETY	It's worrisome.	I don't think I can handle it.	I'm worried about losing it.
FEAR	Get me out of here!	I can't handle it.	I'm losing it.
GRIEF	It's unbearable.	It was too much for me.	I've lost it.
APATHY	I don't care anymore.	I can't do anything.	I can't have anything.
	Complete Abhorrence	**Powerlessness**	**Having Nothing**

Small Portion (about 10%) of the Table of Attitudes (Fig. 3-2)

Good personal work, good relationships, in fact all of the subjects of the Life Skills covered in this book, can have a material affect upon our long term Emotional Scale level.

So much of how we experience life depends upon where we chronically are on the scale. This can scarcely be overrated. We might get into a chicken and egg argument here: which comes first?

1. Good things happen to me and so I feel good, or bad things happen to me so I feel bad. This is a quite commonly held fatalistic view of life that philosophically means that life events cause us to be who and what we are. This one (mechanistic, I want to say behaviorist) is less popular than it used to be.

or:

2. I feel happy and so I tend to see life in such a way as to add to my happiness, or vice versa. Eastern thought would even go so far as to say that by being happy I attract positive things into my life and that if I am in a negative frame of mind, not only will I **see** the world in a more gloomy light, but I will actually attract negative events into my life.

Whether or not you are willing to go that far in accepting causation over your own life and state of well-being, it's clear that whether we are "up" or "down" has a great influence over how we perceive and indeed, experience, the world.

Since our relative position on the Emotional Scale has so much to do with our quality of life, it behooves us to think about ways in which we can raise that relative position, especially as they may affect us in the long term. It's easy to take short term, immediate gratification sorts of actions to "feel good" for a short time. If used as a whole strategy for life, these sorts of actions fall woefully short of providing true quality of life. If only it were that easy! We could just eat/drink/smoke (fill in your favorite vice) our way to happiness and fulfillment. This is one of the more serious problems with the consumer society. It is a frantic race to buy happiness.

Of course it's more complicated than that. Some of the overall best, proven strategies for achieving happiness, fulfillment and excellent quality of life are strategies fraught with peril such as the risks of pain, loss, disappointment and sadness. It hardly seems fair, does it? Consider parenthood for an example. Or shall we say maintaining family relationships of any kind? How about taking the risks involved in starting your own business, or in having any sort of exciting career? Think about it. Excitement = some sort of danger or risk. Life without any excitement might seem like a nice prospect for a while, especially in today's hectic pace, but it soon becomes dull and unappealing.

The apparent alternatives are:

- To choose a path of safe dullness, avoiding as much as possible risks of pain, loss and damage to our self esteem that might cause us to skid down the Emotional Scale.

- Or to dream, take risks, and suffer whatever consequences may befall us.

Looking back to Chapter Two, we can see the importance of having ways to resolve our traumas, hurts and losses. Armed with some good tools for relieving traumatic stress, we do not have to live in fear of it. Equally important, we can be proactive in seeking out personal growth and development of our human potential by continuing to learn and practice methods and subjects that work for us. We can develop our resilience, strength, and consciousness.

> Raising one's consciousness is not always pleasant, especially in the short term. Awareness often increases before ability does.

A woman might realize, painfully, that she has been in the habit of speaking harshly to her friends and employees and hurting their feelings when irritated about anything. Her consciousness has risen to the point where she is now able to perceive something she was not conscious of before in her own behavior. Since this hurts, and makes her feel sad where before she felt fine, it might seem to her like a bad thing, or that she is moving in the wrong direction. In fact, though she has moved down the Emotional Scale at least temporarily, she now has the awareness necessary to work on changing her behavior in a way that could significantly improve the quality of her life.

As another example, a man might realize suddenly that his neglect of his children, even if done for what he sees as a positive motive such as providing them with more material comforts, is hurting the children. As in the example above, he will be likely to feel some pain over this, but the raising of his consciousness gives him the opportunity remedy the situation, improving both his own life and that of his children.

Exercise 3-8: Think of some examples of life situations where awareness comes up first, followed by ability, as someone works on tackling the area of life s/he has now become conscious of.

Exercise 3-9: Either by keeping notes or a journal, if this works for you, or by simple observation:

- **Observe how you feel in your body when you feel good, how your environment looks to you, your sense of your own vibration level, or any other perception that interests you.**

- **Contrast this if you can with times when you are not doing so well or are feeling bad. This may be harder to do since when we feel bad we tend to shut down and withdraw from our environment and our own perceptions to some degree.**

- **Observe some times when you are in a slightly depressed mood from what is normal for you, coming back up to normal, or even higher. (It's generally easier to perceive the coming up phenomena than the going down phenomena.)**

Learning to observe one's own behavior and perceptions as they are happening is a valuable skill. Many people go through life without mastering this, or indeed, without the possibility even occurring to them.

The Predictability Factor

Another way to examine the phenomena of the various Emotional Scale levels is to look at the predictability factor and to put that on a spectrum as well:

At one extreme we have:	In the middle:	At the other extreme:
Low Predictability	**Optimum Predictability**	**High Predictability**
Experienced as stressful to overwhelming.	A good balance between predicted and unpredicted events: large and small.	Experienced as somewhere between boring and deadly dull.

The Predictability Spectrum (Fig. 3-3)

Obviously our environment does have an effect upon us as well as our having an effect upon it. We can be going along, doing just fine, when all of a sudden events can sweep down upon us so fast and with so much impact that we experience them as traumatic. Even if we rise to the occasion and perform very well in the midst of the crisis, the overwhelming nature of the events may catch up with us. We see this, for example, with firefighters, police, and soldiers who do their jobs very well under sometimes horrific conditions but who may suffer the effects later on.

Most trauma occurs on the Low Predictability end of the scale.

- The extreme examples of this are war or large scale natural disasters, where most or all normal familiar structures, both physical and social, break down much faster than they can be repaired.

- Accidents and injuries mostly fall in the middle somewhere, though they can certainly be completely overwhelming to the individual in the moment.

- Less extreme but still potentially traumatic are unfamiliar social situations until one has the chance to meet some people and/or establish something familiar in the environment. A new job, an new school, a new city, any one of these or other similar life changes can give us some discomfort due to predictability in our environment being much lower at first.

Strange, but true, we can also suffer a sort of stress or even pain as a result of things slowing way down and becoming too predictable when we are unable to break out of the pattern. As examples, look at some school experiences, being in prison, or hypothermia. I have seen examples of the high predictability type of trauma in people who were neglected as children, when there was a lack of the human interaction, stimulation and love needed by all young people. In their lives as children it was all too predictable that not much was going to happen. It was a "nothing" where there should have been a "something". Instances of abuse, no matter how bad, are usually easier to address in my experience than is neglect. Traumas caused by a high predictability are harder to get hold of, but there are ways to do it. A major loss, such as loss of a parent (especially when one is a child), loss of a child, or spouse can have an element of this phenomenon as well. The first shock of the loss is usually experienced as too much happening too fast. Once that has passed, the lack of interaction with that lost person sets in. The more a part of one's daily life they were, the greater the loss, as one misses the spontaneous sharing of communication.

So, yes, the environment can impact us and our ability to feel a tolerable or comfortable level of predictability in our environment. Now let's look at how our position on the Emotional Scale affects how we experience predictability. Obviously once you think about it, if we are relatively low on the Emotional Scale, then it takes less unpredictability to overwhelm us.

Exercise 3-10:

Remember a time when you were ill, very tired, or under a lot of stress, and consequently were lower on the Emotional Scale than you normally are.

Observe, looking back, how you responded to predictable and unpredictable events.

An amount of unpredictability that we can easily handle when feeling OK can become an intolerable amount when we are lower on the Emotional Scale. This phenomenon relates to many of the effects of traumatic stress. First we are overwhelmed to some degree by the trauma itself and then, down from our normal level of functioning, we build up more charge and resistance due to not being able to deal as well with the normal stresses of daily life.

When we feel overwhelmed or very uncomfortable with the level of unpredictability in our environment, we tend to retreat and withdraw, which is a survival mechanism (loss of consciousness being an extreme example). If we have a safe place to withdraw to, good support from family and friends, and the chance to re-engage ourselves in living a bit at a time, we may be able to smoothly recover from a difficult period and take up life fully once more. Ha! How often does that happen? Often when we suffer a big trauma or loss, the people around us who we are most counting on for support are suffering too and in need of support themselves. Few of us have the resources to take as much time as we need to optimally recover our strength.

The very least we can do for ourselves is to acknowledge what the situation is. We can realize and acknowledge that either:

1. The volume of unpredictability in our environment is way up, or

2. For whatever reason, our ability to tolerate unpredictability is down.

Just being aware of and understanding the condition can help us not to feel worse. (This is similar to the relief people can feel when they learn that Post-Traumatic Stress Disorder symptoms they have been experiencing are not a sign of their going crazy, but are normal reactions to abnormal experiences.)

On the brighter side, if we are relatively high on the Emotional Scale, not only will we be able to tolerate a higher level of unpredictability, we will take positive action to adjust the level of predictability to suit our preferences. If things get boring, we start something: a conversation, a baseball game, a club, a company. If we find ourselves in a situation that's getting uncomfortably unpredictable, we may back out of the situation for a little to regroup and take action to gradually build up our ability to handle a new level of unpredictability. Thaddeus Golas (*The Lazy Man's Guide to Enlightenment*, 1972) explained time better than I have ever seen it done before, and the relativity of our perception of the speed of time:

"Think of perception as a kind of radar: your wave goes out and bounces back from an object. Needless to say, the facts are more complex than this illustration, but it's close enough to serve.

Let's say someone is shaking a table and a cup is starting to slide off. If your perceptual vibrations are very slow, your waves will give you one message about where the cup is when it starts falling, another flash when it is halfway to the floor, and another when it hits. But if you are vibrating quickly, you will get many messages as the cup starts to fall, telling you the direction it is going, and you will feel as though you have plenty of time to reach over and catch it if you want to."

Exercise 3-11:

Remember a time when you felt confident, happy and productive. Observe, looking back, how you responded to both predicted and unpredicted things.

Using the Emotional Scale to Create Positive Effects

It's possible that you haven't especially considered this before. Maybe you have a philosophy like, "Take people as you find them." Fine and good, but consider for the moment that it may be true that you have the potential power to have a strong good effect on the people in your environment. Of course it's easier for many of us to be pleasant to a grocery store clerk with whom we interact for only a few minutes at a time than it is to maintain positive interaction with close friends and family.

Exercise 3-12:

(Warning – this one can take some guts to look at! It's pretty useless to try to do this one without having first learned to quickly and confidently identify emotional levels.)

As often as you can for the next few days, observe the results of your interactions with clerks and waiters, co-workers, neighbors and friends. Do your best to observe whether people tend to be left in a relatively higher or lower place on the Emotional Scale, or whether there is no change.

Sometimes, when our awareness comes up, we may begin to observe or suspect that we are bringing others down. (We all do it sometimes, such as when we are frustrated or impatient.) In that case, it's time to do some work of our own with someone competent with whom we work well, in order to raise our own chronic emotional level.

Short of that, if you want to try the "pull yourself up by your own bootstraps" approach, using the exercises in this book will tend empower you to become more mobile on the scale. Another thing you can do is to resolve to have a positive effect on your environment to the best of your ability. Despite our best intentions, when we are stuck in a low position on the scale, we are likely to hear quite negative things coming out when we talk. It's hardly to be wondered at. But if we consciously move the focus of our attention from self onto others, it can have an uplifting effect. This is especially true if we learn that we can raise the emotional level of others. If you make the effort to make another's day a bit brighter, yours can't help being brighter too.

Could this practice be used for unscrupulous purposes? Of course it could. "Confidence" people use methods like this to establish trust (a false trust, as it turns out) in their intended victims, the people they are seeking to defraud. That is one reason why it is good to be sensitive to the difference between the social face a person shows the world and the actual chronic Emotional Scale level. Of course, the difference between a person who aims to establish connection and rapport quickly in order to cheat and defraud others, and a person who is establishing connection to brighten another's day, is intention. Practicing this life skill for the joy of having a positive effect on your environment is an entirely different thing from manipulating people.

There are two phases to the practice of using the Emotional Scale to raise another's relative position on it. First is just establishing contact. When you really see and recognize another living being and acknowledge his/her existence, that can cause quite a positive impact in itself, even if you don't know each other. Particularly with the pace and intensity of life these days, people get so wrapped up in themselves and their own concerns that they tend not to take the time to establish real connection with others, especially chance-met people that they may never see again. It goes beyond this. People in cities sometimes form the habit of avoiding eye contact, not talking to strangers, in order to protect their personal space. However, de Becker (1998) notes that we are safer making definite eye contact than we are in avoiding it and appearing timid. For our purpose here, we are connecting just for the sake of connecting.

Recognizing and acknowledging another person is an act of great generosity. It costs you nothing but the small effort to do it. Babies also respond well to this.

Once you have established contact, you can attempt to communicate at the same emotional level as the person, or just a bit higher, and see what will happen. A couple of examples will illustrate this. Once I was in line at a grocery store and the person ahead of me was giving the clerk a very hard time. He was complaining on and on about something. She was doing her best to handle the situation, but he wouldn't be satisfied. As he finally moved on, I caught her eye. I looked up at the ceiling, smiled a little wry smile and shook my head slightly. She brightened right up and smiled gratefully at me. No words were spoken, but because I recognized her and showed that I understood her frustration she was cheered.

When I lived in Los Angeles, there was a little corner store where I'd go several times a week for odds and ends. I've never met a person who the word "curmudgeon" (a grumpy, stubborn person) fit as it did the proprietor of this store. It got to be a game with me to see if I could brighten him up. After weeks of sunshine we'd have a little bit of rain. I'd say to him, "Lousy weather!" And he'd answer, "Right!" and go off into a cheerful grumble about how, "You can't depend on anything."

A wonderful example of this kind of duplication comes from Stephanie, my daughter. She was caring for a toddler who got into a raging tantrum—the sort of situation where normal communication is impossible. She picked him up and carried him to a mirror. He was raging, crying, and holding his body as stiff as board. She held him up to the mirror and, remembering back to upsets from her own childhood, she duplicated exactly the expression on his face. She looked him in the eye (via the mirror) with no intention to criticize him or make him wrong. She said, "I know how you feel". He cried for another minute or two and then his attention shifted to something else and he became cheerful and interested in his surroundings.

Studying and playing with this material showed me that we often come at each other with an attitude like, "You shouldn't feel that way" towards other people. The fact that that approach never works doesn't stop us from doing it. Playing this Emotional Scale game works so much better. When we say to another in essence, "I see that this is how you feel," the acknowledgement of how they feel is often enough to release them from it or from the seriousness of it, at least for a time. (I had been practicing this for years before I encountered the work of Marshall Rosenberg, author of *Non-Violent Communication*, 1999 which covers this same phenomenon.)

These exercises are meant to be done with strangers or acquaintances. Of course you can use your understanding of the Emotional Scale in your relationships with friends and intimates as well. (The next chapter is especially relevant for the purpose of improving long term relationships.)

Exercise 3-13:

1. Making a conscious decision to do this with people you encounter for the next few days:

- **If possible, take note of a person as you approach him or her.**
- **See what you are able to observe about his or her emotional level.**
- **Look the person right in the eye (if possible/appropriate).**
- **Say hello (or a similar greeting).**
- **Smile, unless the person seems to be in an emotional state that makes that inappropriate.**

2. **Once you have established contact, make a remark about the weather or some such topic, doing the best you can to match the Emotional Scale level of the other person or just a bit above it, and observe the result.**

If you "miss", it is not a big deal. You will improve with practice. If you get it right, the other person will usually brighten up, at least a little. It costs little effort to become adept at establishing a connection with another human being in a short period of time.

Chapter Summary

The Emotional Scale is the spectrum of emotions from low to high. They range from slow and heavy near the bottom to light, fast, and free-flowing near the top.

A person's chronic Emotional Scale is where the person "lives". It is his or her default band on the scale. An acute (temporary, in the moment) emotional level is caused events or influences in the environment, including the person's own mental world. Despite outside influences, a person has a strong tendency to revert to his/her chronic emotional level unless effective work is done or some profound change occurs in the person's life.

Though people and pressures, both positive and negative, in our environment can have an influence on our emotional state, there is a lot we can do to positively affect our own emotional level once we are aware of the phenomena of the Emotional Scale.

Familiarity with the scale allows us to understand and predict human attitudes and behaviors substantially.

Finally, knowing the Emotional Scale gives us the means to cause positive effects on the people around us, from those we know well to complete strangers.

4 Understanding & Improving Relationships

- Communion: A Theory of Relatedness
- Understanding the Components of Relatedness
- Building Relationship
- Types of Connection
- Repairing Breakdowns

Communion: A Theory of Relatedness

I saw the Dalai Lama when he came to visit Ann Arbor in April 1994. There was great anticipation of his visit and of the words of wisdom he would share in his public appearances. I was fortunate enough to be able to attend one of his lectures and I remember the hush over the large crowd as he walked on stage. What did he tell us? What did the newspapers report about each of his talks here in Ann Arbor? He told us, "Be kind to each other." Of course he said much more in his gentle and eloquent way, but that was the essence of his message, "Be kind to each other."

I could feel the response from some of the audience that day, "Is that all?" But when you think about it, being kind to each other is not only a virtue and an ideal, but a life's work. *Many* things are easier than the practice of daily kindness to those around us. Anything that helps us in this practice is a useful tool for life. Such practice helps us to strengthen our characters and help us to improve the quality, not only of our own lives, but of all those whose lives touch ours.

Of course, human beings are capable of great kindness, even heroic kindness to others, especially when disaster strikes. While that is admirable for sure, what may be harder in some ways is sustained kindness to those around us day after day.

What we will be looking at in this chapter is raising the level of positive connection between people in daily life.

Understanding the Components of Relationship

Now I want to share with you one of my favorite parts of Applied Metapsychology. Dr. Gerbode's model for understanding relationships can be applied both in sessions with clients and in daily life. If you draw a circle and write around the outside edge: *Communication, Comprehension, Affection,* and then write inside the circle: *Communion,* you will have the basic model. He uses the word *communion,* not in its religious sense obviously, but more in the sense of, "a possessing or sharing in common, participation; a sharing of thoughts or feelings."

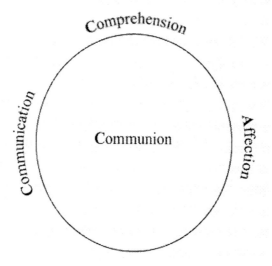

A Model for Communion (Fig. 4-1)

A lot passes for *Communication* that really isn't, if we define communication as the interchange of ideas, concepts and feelings, with the message sent across by the sender being accurately received by the receiver. (As one of my students on an Effective Communication Workshop once said, "Oh, you mean *real* communication!") *Comprehension* refers not just to the understanding of a particular message or communication, but also to the wider context of a common ground or shared frame of reference. *Affection* is the degree of liking between people; it is an attractive force. If affection is high, you want that person near you and may even feel close when physically far apart. Low affection can have a repelling force to it. If you don't like someone or are upset with someone you ordinarily do like, you wish them far away. Communion then is the sum of these parts, a word that represents the quality of connection between people.

Building Relationship

Communication is where we commonly start when meeting someone new. We exchange ideas by communicating to find out if we have some sort of common ground, a basis for a relationship. We achieve comprehension of each other by this exchange. We may both be interested in gardening for instance, and even though we might have quite differing views on proper gardening methods, we could settle down to arguing about this happily. As we establish some comprehension between us, we usually start to feel some affection and wish to communicate more. In this way communion rises.

Sometimes we can go from comprehension as a starting point. If you attend a lecture on a subject that particularly interests you, even if you are shy, you may find it easier to strike up a conversation with a stranger sitting nearby. This is because you can assume that that person's presence at the lecture shows a similar interest to your own. The comprehension in that situation is already there, making it easier to start communicating.

Once in a while we meet someone we like immediately, even before we have a chance to communicate and establish some comprehension. We meet a person and just instantly like him or her without even knowing who s/he is yet. No matter which of the parts of communion seem to come first, each leads to more of each of the other parts, allowing communion to blossom and grow.

Exercise 4-1:

- Remember some times when you entered into communion with someone through communication.

- Remember some times when you entered into communion with someone through a background of comprehension.

- Remember some times when you entered into communion with someone through instant affection.

- Repeat each item as long as you are interested or until you have a positive shift.

Types of Connection

At the European Metapsychology Conference of November 2001 held in Milan, an interesting distinction came up in discussion: that we cannot fully understand communion until we distinguish three specific types:

- Social Communion
- One-Way Communion
- Two-Way Communion

Social Communion

A type of communion we might call *social communion* occurs when two people talk as acquaintances without exchanging any deeply felt beliefs or emotions. This sort of interchange can be very pleasant without being especially deep. Social communion is the appropriate level in many social and work situations. Communication at this level may be testing the waters for the possibility of deeper communion, or our interchange with that person may continue in the social communion vein.

We have countless opportunities for striking up social communion with people we encounter. Some we will never see again; others we may meet up with repeatedly for brief non-intense social interaction. Of course, some people we meet up with may not want to communicate, or to enter into communion, even the social kind. It's important to respect this. You can always "float" a communication over to someone and wait to see what the response will be. An initial communication is an invitation to the other to enter into communion.

If the invitation is accepted because the "invitee" is ready and willing to communicate, you can go on from there to build some communion. (The exercises given near the end of the last chapter have as much to do with establishing and building communion as they do with the Emotional Scale. You might wish to revisit them with this in mind.)

Exercise 4-2:

- **Practice establishing and building communion with people as you go through the day. Practice your ability to communicate something that will be real (comprehensible) to the other person and engage his/her willingness to communicate further.**

- **This is a social skill that we all have to a greater or lesser degree. Consciously practicing the ability just puts in more in your command.**

- **Try this either verbally or non-verbally with babies.**

One-Way Communion

Another type of communion we may call *one-way communion*. This occurs in the relationships between professional people and their patients or clients. We expect from doctors, dentists, lawyers, counselors and therapists that they will listen compassionately to our problems and offer the appropriate treatment or service, without their taking a turn to unload any similar problems they might have upon us. That is one-way communion. The relationship may be quite cordial and friendly and marked by significant communion (by definition, a phenomenon between people that both are experiencing), but the communication is one-way in the sense that though two people are involved in the communication, only one of them gets to share personal thoughts, feelings, etc.

This is really why "dual relationships" (friendship or romance or business relationships between a professional person and his or her patient or client) are frowned upon. It can be difficult to maintain the boundaries of the one-way professional relationship while also having another (two-way) relationship with the same person. Also the professional in the relationship elicits a feeling of trust and safety in the client as a result of the practice of this one-way communion that can give him or her an unfair advantage if the relationship moves into a deeper degree of communion. A person on the receiving end of a one-way relationship, a counseling client let us say, usually shares thoughts, feelings and concerns with the other person at a deeper level and faster than in a two-way relationship where trust is built up more slowly. The position of trust the professional person has upon entering into this one-way communication allows a deeper, faster intimacy, even though it only goes one way. As the client relaxes into the safety of this trust, it can be such a relief and (if the professional is doing a good job) the client can feel so well understood that the common "falling in love with" one's therapist, medical doctor, (fill in the profession), phenomenon can occur. The communion experienced in these situations is real and is appropriate as long as the professional person maintains professional boundaries. In terms of normal human relationships, it is artificial in that it is one-way communication. Looking at it from the other side, professional people receive this relatively swift, deep trust and admiration from their clients due to the special nature of the relationship. This aspect of one-way communication can lead to a professional feeling that s/he is falling in love with a client.

We might just call that one-way type of communion "professional communion" except for the fact that it is necessary in some other contexts as well. In communicating with a child, an adult needs to understand that he or she has the overall responsibility for the quality of the communion. According to Woititz (*Healthy Parenting*, 1992), the needs of the child come first. Parents who lean on a child for emotional support, or for someone to listen to their troubles are behaving inappropriately. Children need the support of this one-way communion in order to develop with relative smoothness into fully responsible adults themselves. Of course the love between parent and child flows both ways, and each can communicate with the other and achieve comprehension. What is one-way is the responsibility for the relationship overall, and the care the parent takes in all aspects of communion to fulfill that responsibility. (My sister Jennifer points out that a great source of frustration in parent-child relationships comes from parents resisting a shift from the one-way to the two-way form of communion as their children enter adulthood.)

Another example of the need for the uneven type responsibility in a relationship occurs when one of the people is unable due to his or her mental, physical or emotional condition to assume an equal responsibility. Someone who is in horrendous physical pain, or who is undergoing great mental or emotional stress, whether from some situation in life or from a chronic mental condition, will be less likely to be able to shoulder equal responsibility for the quality of communication. Friends often give each other turns to be the one who needs some extra care or consideration. Such things as serious business difficulties, or severe illness, put a strain on relationships and families. Couples and families who understand this and manage it well can survive crises, or even come through them stronger than before. Couples and families who do not understand and work with this can crack under the strain. (Wallerstein and Blakesley, *The Good Marriage*, 1996).

It's a special ability to be completely able receive and appreciate the communication, comprehension (at whatever level it may be) and affection from another person you are in an unequal relationship with, without any resentment of the inequality. Most people manage it at least part of the time with their own children.

Exercise 4-3:

1. **Remember a time when you experienced good one-way communion with a professional person such as a doctor, therapist, etc.**
   What was that experience like?

2. **Remember a time when you were in a one-way communion situation with a professional person that did not go well.**
   What happened?

   Was something missing?

• **Repeat steps 1-2 as long as you are interested**

Exercise 4-4:

1. Remember a time when you, as a professional person, parent, friend of a person in need, etc., achieved good one-way communion with another. What was that experience like?

2. Remember when you, as a professional person, parent, etc., were in one-way communion with someone when it did not go well.

   What happened?

   Was something missing?

- Repeat steps 1-2 as long as you are interested.

Two-Way Communion

Now let's move on from social and one-way communion to something that is two-way and a bit deeper. With people we spend more time with, friends, co-workers, business associates or colleagues, we have the opportunity to build communion that is more meaningful because we share more. Communion grows and becomes more rewarding as we establish habits of communication, common purposes and easy affection with these people. In our more intimate relationships, we can have communion deep and true. Good family relationships and good close friendships provide deep affection that has grown over the years of knowing and being known at the deepest level, the familiarity that only comes with shared experience, good memories and lots and lots of communication. While people who experience love at first sight, or who meet and become instant close friends, have that sense of knowing each other deeply, there is still the work to do (and delightful work it is), of filling in the comprehension by means of lots of communication. Getting to know another in all of his/her facets and qualities just does take some time.

Some people who fear or avoid intimate relationships and who would be uncomfortable with deep communion, are adept at social communion. Such people feel safe in the very limitations of social communion and its relative anonymity. On the other hand, some people who are comfortable in deep communion in familiar close relationships are fearful of communion with strangers and are awkward and shy with new people. It isn't an either/or proposition. It is just an interesting set of phenomena in that we might tend to think that someone who is "good at" communion in one context would also be comfortable in another.

> Communion with others is perhaps the best reward of living.

Ideally a person can be at home in the world and can go anywhere and strike up some level of communion with the people s/he finds there. If no kindred spirits appear, the communion stays on the social level. Once s/he finds a congenial person, communion can deepen quite rapidly into true friendship.

For optimum quality of life, we want to be adept at *all* forms of communion:

- Social communion.

- One-way Communion.

- Two-way Communion between people on an equal basis.

Our ability to commune relates to the Emotional Scale since, higher on the scale, people tend to be more able to experience and generate the components of communion. Each of these separate skills has impact on the quality of life:

- Ability to enter into social communion in all sorts of situations.

- Ability to maintain social communion over time.

- Ability to establish communion on either side of an unequally based communion.

- Ability to maintain communion on either side of an unequal relationship.

- Ability to enter into strong, deep communion.

- Ability to maintain close communion over time.

Exercise 4-5:

Do these exercises over a period of some days or weeks. If doing them alone, you can keep track of your practice and the results in a journal. If working with a partner or in a group, you will probably want to discuss these exercises over some weeks.

1. Think of some ways to establish social communion with new acquaintances, or to build social communion with people you already know. Choose one or two of these and practice them. Notice the results.

2. Think of some ways to establish or build one-way communion, either on the receiving side or the cause side, or both. Choose one or two of these. Notice the results.

3. Think of some ways to build communion with your nearest and dearest. If you are willing, choose one or two of these and put them into practice. Notice the results.

Why would anyone not want to improve communion with his/her intimates? Vulnerability is a key component in intimacy. Intimacy is all about opening up to another person, and this can be scary for many people. Notice whether any reluctance, resistance or any other feelings or attitudes come up for you when you contemplate building communion with the people closest to you. The next section may shed some light on anything that comes up. Our fears about being vulnerable come from misunderstandings, hurts and upsets in the past. Doing good work in session can clear up loads of charge on past upsets. Meanwhile, we can become skilled at cleaning up upsets as they occur.

Repairing Breakdowns

Now that we have looked at the component parts of communion and how they build together, let's look at what happens in an upset, a breakdown of communion. Just as all the parts build together, when one part breaks down, all the rest are dragged down as well. For example if you are meeting me for lunch at a restaurant and I am late, you may be tolerant at first. As time goes on your tolerance may wear thin and eventually you get upset. There is no communication so you don't know what is going on (= no comprehension) and whenever an upset occurs, affection drops. If I finally do show up, your first feeling will probably be that you do not want to talk to me! That is the normal response to broken communion. Of course, the correct thing to do is to communicate in spite of that. With communication re-established, comprehension can come back (maybe I had a flat tire on the way to the restaurant) and affection rekindles.

It is essential to realize that communion has to exist before it can be broken. When it breaks (and the stronger the communion was between two people, the bigger the upset will be when it breaks), there is a tendency to think that it really wasn't there at all. Let's look at a balloon as an analogy. If you stick a pin into a balloon that has very little air in it, not much happens. If you stick the pin into a balloon that is fairly well filled with air, you will get a pop. With a very tightly filled balloon, a pin prick will make a much louder bang. The more communion present, the bigger the "bang" when it breaks. The effect of a communion break is to invalidate the communion that has gone before. If you keep that in mind, you can overcome the normal tendency to want to withhold communication from a person with whom you are upset.

Here is a story that illustrates the point that communion has to exist before it can be broken. I had a boyfriend once who took me home to meet his parents. Over dinner, my boyfriend and his father started complaining about the other son in the family who had moved away and stopped communicating with them. They were saying lots of disparaging things about him, and one might have thought that they never wanted to see him again. After dinner I took the mother aside and asked her for her other son's address while my boyfriend and his father were off doing something else. She was perfectly willing to give it to me even though she had just met me. Mothers are almost always the last to give up on their children. Then I wrote to the brother and said, "You don't know me; I'm your brother's girlfriend. I'm writing to tell you that I can see that your father and your brother love you very much. The reason I know this is because they are very upset that you are not communicating with them. I just wanted to let you know this in case you want to get back in touch with them." It worked! He did get back in touch with his family, apparently in response to my letter, and that was the end of all the complaints about what a terrible person he was.

When two people have an upset and do the work of fully repairing it, the relationship is stronger than before, similar to a broken bone that has healed. Good relationships do not depend on never having any upsets; that would be unreal. Good relationships do depend on a high level of trust. Trust gets strengthened every time a break in communion is repaired. Although there are three components, there are just two main strategies for repairing breakdowns:

1. Naming the type of breakdown reduces the charge it generates. For example, two friends can sit down together and sort out how a misunderstanding happened from each person's point of view until full understanding is reached and communion is restored. One might say, "For me it was a break in comprehension because I didn't understand what was going on with you when you walked away without talking to me." The other might say, "Well that's interesting. I can see how you felt that way. For me it was a break in affection because I didn't think you cared about talking to me because you were talking to George for so long while I was waiting to talk to you!" In this way, being respectful of each other's feelings, the two can repair their communion. (Sometimes one person or both will need a cooling-off period before effective communication can take place.) This strategy employs the use of communication to re-establish comprehension and hence restore the communion.

2. The other strategy uses straight affection. With this approach the individuals simply let go of or "get off" their disagreements and misunderstandings and reassert their affection for each other. John Gottman (*The Seven Principles that Make Marriage Work*, 2000), advocates this method over the "communicate it out" approach.

Though it is not true in all cases, women tend to favor the first method over the second and men tend to prefer the second over the first. At least, with this data in mind, two people with different styles can take a look at their preferences and gain understanding of what is happening.

Sometimes there is too much upset occurring for either of these strategies to work. One or both of the people need to work on it with a facilitator or counselor, either individually, or in joint sessions. Often earlier breakdowns, including ones that happened in earlier relationships, are tied in to current one and those need to be resolved to fully handle the current situation. Keeping this in mind can help us to be more tolerant of self and others. Whenever a person's current upset fails to resolve, it is tied to an earlier one.

My father pointed out to me that if you are in a general state of broken down communion in most areas of life, then life can occur for you as so flat, dull and gray that another upset hardly makes much impact, but just adds to the general gloom. Once you have increased your communion however, from clearing up or letting go of past upsets, when you are clean and sparkly and wide open to communication, comprehension and affection, then a disruption is intolerable. It is something that must be resolved immediately if possible because it is too painful to tolerate.

Exercises 4-6:

1. **A. Think of a time when an upset that you had or that you observed was not fully healed. Was there a lasting effect from that upset?**

   B. Think of a time when an upset you had or that you observed was fully healed with the communion restored to its former level or even higher.

   C. Repeat as long as you are interested.

2. **Enlisting the willingness of a friend or mate, try both strategies for repairing communion breaks as the opportunity arises. Compare notes on what works or doesn't work for you as a pair.**

There are a number of misconceptions about love, communion and relationships floating around in the world. One is the idea that falling in love is the peak of a love relationship and that it's all downhill from there. Not true. Over time as people work through their upsets and continue to build communion, their closeness grows and gets richer. Another is the idea that love just dies for no reason, the "falling out of love" phenomenon. In this case, there are many, many large or small breaks in communion which have not been resolved and eventually build up to the point where one or both of the people in the relationship can't stand it any more.

Another false idea is that a break has to weaken a relationship of any kind. If you and your friend have a big upset and manage to work all the way through it to complete understanding, harmony and restored communion, the relationship and the trust will be stronger than ever, just as a broken bone when it heals grows stronger in the broken place.

Another application of the concept of communion in everyday experience is to use it as an indicator of how well we are doing in life. The level of communion we feel for ourselves, our bodies, our environment, and the people around us, has everything to do with our quality of life. A life filled with upsets, withheld communication and resentments is not very much fun. A life warm with communion, both the social kind and true deep communion, is rewarding indeed. We can use the concept as an indicator or guide when making life decisions: will the outcome be less communion, or more and better communion? We can use the concept to examine and improve our own behavior by looking at how our words and actions affect the level of communion between ourselves and others.

> Applying this model in life is kindness in action.

Chapter Summary

Gerbode's model: Communication + Comprehension + Affection = Communion, makes sense of the components of relationship. Once we understand each one and see how these necessary ingredients affect each other, we have useful knowledge for building our connections with other people.

This connection may be:

Social, which is to say the kind of connection we have in the course of daily life with people we do not know or know only slightly, or in the context of business.

- One-way, when one person bears all or most of the responsibility for the relationship, for example:

  - Parent and child.
  - Professional person and client.
  - Anyone and a person who is very needy (either chronically or acutely).

- Two-way, Communion between equals who know each other. In this category we find Communion in its deepest and most profound form.

Knowing how to build relationship and connectedness also gives us insight into how breaks in Communion may be repaired. This helps our chances having relationships that grow better and stronger through the years.

<table>
<tr><td>

5
</td><td>

A Useful
Life Model
</td><td>

</td></tr>
</table>

- The Domains: Spheres of Influence and Responsibility
- Domains of Consciousness
- Balance: How Domains and Aspects of Domains Affect Each Other
- Collapse and Inversion of the Domains
- Decision Making As Informed by Domains
- Lining Up the Domains

The Domains: Spheres of Influence and Responsibility

I remember in a philosophy class in college encountering Utilitarianism with its concept of the greatest good for the greatest number. I remember thinking, "That's pretty good." Though it certainly is an advance over only using what is good for oneself as an operating basis, I wasn't entirely satisfied with it. I didn't see a way then to improve upon it, but years later when I met Dr. Gerbode and we discussed his model of domains, I found it to be a superior way of for thinking about: "What is right?" "What is good?" and "Why is that so?"

The domains provide a method of looking at life, for improving quality of life, and for making decisions so as to bring about the greatest good for the greatest number of these domains. Since becoming familiar with Gerbode's concept of domains, I have seen several other notions of basically the same idea, most notably one by the philosopher Sam Keen (*Passionate Life: Stages of Loving*, 1983).

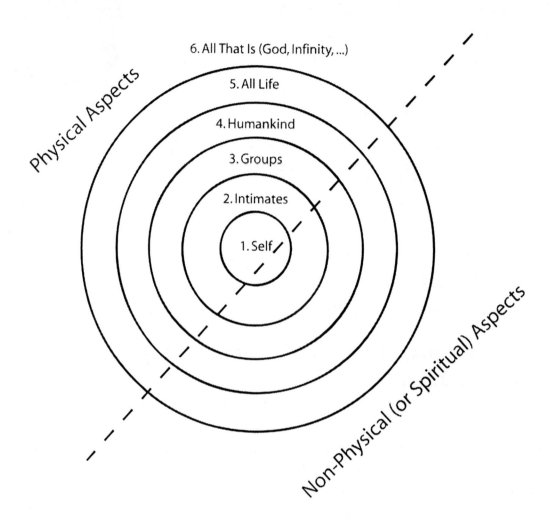

The Domains (Fig. 5-1)

Gerbode defines a life *domain* as a sphere of influence or responsibility including all of the activities, duties, and personal identities of that area of life.

The domains can most easily be depicted as a series of concentric circles:

- Because we use the person-centered viewpoint, we have the Self in the center as the First Domain.

- The Second Domain is Intimates, which includes all of those people to whom you feel especially close. This usually (but not always) includes family, parents, mate, children, close friends and sometimes extended family. For some people, members of other species form part of their second and third domains.

- Moving outward from the Intimates Domain we have Groups, which are looser associations than the ones we are calling Intimates. A Group could be as small as two people united for some common purpose or as large as a race or a nation. Most groups we deal with on a regular basis fall somewhere in between. Larger and smaller groups at school, at work or in the neighborhood, are all usually united by a common purpose or identity.

- Enclosing all human groups of all kinds is our species, the Humankind Domain. (If we were another species, our Fourth Domain would be the totality of that species).

- Humankind is included within the Fifth Domain, All Life, all of the plants and animals on the planet. (Hmm, that brings up an interesting point. If we were aware of life on other planets, would all that life fit into the fifth domain, or would we need to put in a new one, a planetary domain? Good question! We'll save that for another time...)

- The Sixth Domain is God, the Universe, Infinity, All That Is, or whatever you consider this to be, that which includes all other domains.

In my early discussions with Dr. Gerbode on these domains, I suggested to him that there are two aspects to each domain. In Fig. 5-1, you will see that there is a dotted line down through the center of concentric circles. This represents the fact that there is both a physical and a non-physical (spiritual, if you will) aspect to each domain. Another way to say this is that there is both a subjective and an objective aspect to each domain. One need not have any spiritual beliefs to see the two different aspects.

The First Domain – Self

Starting with yourself, on the physical side you have your body and all of your possessions. On the non-physical side you have your mind, thoughts, emotions, plans, dreams and your personality, all of those intangibles that go into making you unique. For those to whom this is real, you as a spiritual being also belong on this intangible side. Of course each domain is not subdivided into physical and non-physical, but plotting it out this way allows us to examine and work with life more effectively.

The Second Domain – Intimates

On the Second Domain are the people you are closest to, usually the people you live with, whether they be family or friends, and those people you most like to spend time with and who you hold most dear. On the physical side is your home, if you share it with others, the physical bodies of the people you class as intimates, and any other physical property you own together or share. On the non-physical side are the individual personalities of the people involved, plus the unique relationships they form between them. Included here are love and other feelings, and the hopes and dreams shared by any group of intimates, small or large.

Judith Wallerstein (*The Good Marriage*, 1996) discovered in her research that couples who have successful long lasting marriages pay attention to the well-being of the relationship itself, as if it were a living entity, not just to the individual people within the relationship. This is probably true of all long-lasting groups of intimates.

The Third Domain – Groups

The Third Domain encompasses all sorts of groups, from fairly close and tight (but outside the realm of Intimates), to very large and amorphous. Groups of people in work, social and neighborhood contexts belong in this domain. In a work situation, people are united by a common purpose, such as to manufacture widgets, or, more likely, to make a living. There can be a great range of difference in the amount of group-feeling in groups at work, from sullen disconnectedness to uplifting camaraderie and team spirit. Groups have positions on the Emotional

Scale as well as individuals do. The spirit and flavor of a group has a lot to do with its leadership (and that would be the *actual*, not necessarily the titular leadership.)

Social groups may form around a specific purpose such as dancing, playing bridge, a sport, or stamp collecting. Other social groups are just people who enjoy being together, no matter what it is that they are doing. As for neighborhoods, if yours is like many, it may not be much of a group at all. Unless it is an intentional community, people in a neighborhood often have little in common with each other besides having moved into the same area. In times before rapid transportation, people socialized with their neighbors as a matter of course, but that is no longer true. Often it takes some outside force such as the fallout of severe weather to bring neighbors together in a group effort.

We can go as far out with this Group Domain as considering a city or state, a race or nation as a group. People sometimes consider themselves to be part of such a large group when it is threatened. Such large groups are so diverse that their only common purpose may be to survive as a race or nation. Once we move out this far it can get harder to think about in personal terms, unlike our smaller groups and our intimates. Something like the Olympics raises people's awareness of national identity.

The Fourth Domain – Humankind

The next domain moving outward is the whole of humanity, the Humankind Domain. On the physical side of this domain we have the bodies of all the human beings, plus all of the human artifacts that we have constructed: roads, bridges, buildings, works of art, etc. On the non-physical side are the personalities/beings of all the individual humans, plus the common intention to survive as a species. Often human beings are so busy squabbling among themselves that they don't give a lot of thought or attention to this Fourth Domain, their species. A common theme in science fiction is an attack or invasion from another planet. Such an event might well cause Humankind to pull itself together as never before, at least for a time, to counter this threat. One area where human beings have tended to see themselves as united is against the wild, natural world. In earlier times when we were spread thin over the earth and large predators roamed the world, the need to stick together was more apparent. However, history shows us that there have always been wars. Currently, many people identify with the struggle toward a sustainable future, for world peace and similar large scale goals.

As it happens, there *is* a threat to all human life on this planet, but because it not something that is as readily visible as alien invaders would be, only some individuals and groups can perceive it as yet.

Meanwhile, the Information Age, telecommunication and most recently the Internet, have brought humanity closer together than at any time in recorded history. It will be fascinating to see what develops from here.[3]

One great event has raised human awareness of both the fourth and fifth domains. R. Buckminster Fuller and others have noted that once someone got far enough off the planet's surface during space exploration to send back a picture of our beautiful, finite sphere, human consciousness was changed forever. This is it. This is where we have to live – all of us and all of the countless other species that make life on planet Earth what it is. Standing on the surface of the planet, from the perspective of a single human being, the planet looks endlessly huge. It took a picture from space to show us its wholeness, its oneness, and its relative smallness.

"Earthrise" as seen from
Apollo 8 capsule
(Christmas 1968)
NASA file photo

---

[3] Check out my online book list for more information, especially Russell, Sheldrake and Wright. See Appendix B.

The Fifth Domain – All Life

While people have always been aware of the physical bodies of animals and plants, usually to the exclusion of anything significant on the non-physical side, indigenous cultures have maintained the awareness of the spirit, if you will, of other life forms, other species, than our own. The developed world has only relatively recently begun to be conscious of the non-physical aspect of the Fifth Domain (besides us humans, that is).

In my opinion, we have only begun to scratch the surface of consciousness in relation to other living things (a particular interest of mine) and life as a whole on this planet.

The Sixth Domain – All That Is

Notice that the dotted line does not go out to the edge of the page in Fig. 5-1. That is to show that All That Is encompasses everything, both physical and non-physical. What is it all about? What are we here for? What is the meaning of life? We might have a fascinating discussion about God, the Universe, and Everything. Is it conscious of itself? If it is, what is it doing/thinking/feeling? Human beings have very different sets of beliefs about this domain. Some think that the universe is just a phenomenon, not conscious of anything. Some think that it is a phenomenon created by a Supreme Being. Some think that the Universe itself is aware and alive, and that we create it as it supports and creates us. To get back to the practical matters of life skills, let's look at how consciousness of the domains affects life.

Exercise 5-1:

On a large piece of paper, map out your Domains, making sure to include the physical and non-physical aspects of each. Make it as complete as you can. Some people like to use photographs or draw pictures to illustrate their Domains.

If you are working with another person or in a group, show and explain your Domains to someone else. Let them tell you about their Domains.

Exercise 5-2:

For practice, if it amuses you, try writing out the component parts of the domains of someone else that you know. For a real challenge, look at the domains of a member of another species.

Exercise 5-3:

Part 1.

- Think of a Second Domain, a group of Intimates (2 or more people) that you have been a part of or that you have observed, that was not surviving well.

- What, if anything, was working well?

- What was not working?

- Are there any other things you can observe about the dynamics of that set of Intimates?

Part 2.

- Now think of a set of Intimates that you have been a part of or that you have observed that was surviving well.

- What, if anything, was not working well?

- What were these people doing that was working well?

- Are there any other things you can observe about the dynamics of that set of Intimates?

Repeat 1 & 2 as often as you like – for as long as you are interested or until you get some sort of a positive shift.

Now do the same as above for the Third Domain, which is Groups.

If you are interested in taking a look at the other Domains with this Exercise, do so (even though you really have only one Fourth, Fifth and Sixth Domain to choose from, so it will go a bit differently.)

Domains of Consciousness

Certainly there is conscious awareness (which is to say: aware, and aware of being aware), at the level of the First Domain. The study of child development is largely the study of how human consciousness develops from infancy onward.[4] Some human beings make it through these stages of development to arrive at full adult awareness. Others get stuck along the road and have to struggle through life with an immature degree of awareness. In any case, an individual who is functioning at all has some awareness of self.

There is conscious awareness among the members of a family that they are, indeed a family (for better or worse). A group of intimates is aware of their identity as a close-knit group. Once we get to the Third Domain we find some people, and some groups, with a strong awareness of group-ness. Real leadership is good for that, both for making individual members of a group feel acknowledged for themselves and for bringing about awareness of the living entity that is the group. Awareness of this domain can be fairly shaky, especially without good leadership. Many people work for a company or with other people with little sense of the group as a whole. If you look at a company as if it were an organism, it is easy to see that it has needs. It produces something: some product or service, to exchange with the outside world in order to get what it needs. The organism may be in good or in poor health, just as an animal or a person might be.

Lack of conscious awareness of the reality of a domain is what allows a person to cheat on her life partner or to steal from the company he works for, not seeing that these actions harm self as well. The less conscious awareness any domain has the less ability it will have:

- To see to its own well-being and that of its members.
- To act with intelligence and integrity.
- To shape its own destiny.

This is true whether we are talking about an individual, a couple, a family, a group of friends, a company, a nation or a species.

---

[4] See online book list, especially Weinhold & Weinhold

At the Third Domain, it is no wonder that that things can get a bit fuzzy, as the individual may feel pulled this way and that by sometimes conflicting loyalties. At the Fourth Domain is where most people seem to lose it in terms of conscious awareness of ourselves as the domain of the human species.

Art and science help us to transcend our limitations and divisions. Musicians and artists communicate across language barriers. Scientists and mathematicians, who are more interested in their studies and discoveries than they are in politics, always find ways to communicate with each other around the world. We might see these things as bridges toward Fourth Domain (Humankind) awareness as a whole.

Let us imagine that full conscious awareness is possible at every level. Not just *my* domains: my body, my house, my family, my friends, my company, my country, my plants, my pets, and my religion or spirituality. Not just *your* domains: your body, your house, your family, your friends, your company, your country, your plants, your pets, and your religion or spirituality. But *the* domains – you and I as individuals, each of our collections of intimates and groups, and all the groups everywhere, all of the human beings, and all life, every living thing – all the physical material of our world, and all of its non-physical phenomena. This sort of expansion of consciousness is the basis of transcendent experience.

Meanwhile, back at home, the point is that if we really consider each domain, both our own personal domains and the total of each domain, we have a much better chance of surviving well as individuals, families, groups, humankind, and as a part of all the life on this planet.

Balance: How Domains and Aspects of Domains Affect Each Other

Now let us consider how this model can be used as a practical ethical philosophy. We're going to look at balance now, both balance between the physical and non-physical sides of each domain, and across all of one's personal domains.

Some people are way over-balanced in the direction of physical well-being, providing material comforts for themselves and their families, but paying little or no attention to mental/emotional/spiritual (non-physical) needs. This engenders the truism that money doesn't buy happiness. Other people are way over-balanced in the other direction, thinking great thoughts and having great philosophical discussions while the dishes go unwashed and the bills unpaid. Ideal survival involves balance across both aspects of the domains.

Exercise 5-4:

1. Think of a situation where someone you know or know about has been concentrating on the physical side of survival to the detriment of the non-physical aspects of life.

- **What did this look like? To what extent did it seem to work?**

- **What were the consequences of neglecting the other side of the person's domains?**

2. Think about a situation where someone you know or know about has been concentrating on the non-physical aspects of the domains to the detriment of physical well-being.

- **What did this look like? To what extent did it seem to work?**

- **What were the consequences of neglecting the other side of the person's domains?**

- **Repeat part 2 as long as you are interested or until you get a positive shift.**

When we look at all of the domains and all of the demands and complexity contained therein, life can appear to be a juggling act at best, or like the circus act where someone spins plates on sticks. Change is inevitable. As long as you are alive, things are changing in you and around you. You just get one area of life going well and it seems another area claims your attention. One domain, or portion of a domain, in crisis can take up so much energy that it can seem to suck the life out of the others, at least for a time.

My late husband died when our daughter was just three and a half years old. I coped through the immediate loss alright, but many things crashed in over time:

my feelings of failure in that relationship, the difficulties of being a single parent, relative financial disaster for a time. Life seemed to go on as before, but I was closed in upon myself to a greater degree than I realized. During this time I neglected my relationships with my mother and daughter. It wasn't until many months later when I finally pulled myself and my domains together that I could look back and see how closed in I had been. No matter how 'normal' it is considered to be to go through things like that with a significant loss, it was useful to me to look at the effects of that loss on all the rest of my domains.

Personal illness or illness in a family member, a drug or alcohol problem, any big loss of relationship or position, a financial reversal, all these sorts of things can cause a loss of well-being of one's domains. Being aware of this when it happens, as aware as possible, helps us to allow time and space to deal with the crisis and then to remember to spread our attention back out through our domains once the crisis has passed.

Exercise 5-5:

1. A. Think of a time when some aspect of your First Domain was in crisis and pulled down your other domains.

    - How did you cope?

    - Did there come a time when you were able to spread your attention back out through your domains?

    B. Think of a time when some aspect of your First Domain was doing so well that it spilled over into your other domains with a positive effect.

    - What effects did that have?

    C. Repeat as long as you are interested or until you get a positive shift.

2. Repeat the above exercise using the Second Domain (Intimates), Third Domain (Groups), Fourth Domain (Humankind), and Fifth Domain (All Life), if you are interested.

On the positive side of the equation, a great surge in well-being on one domain can positively affect the rest of the domains. Getting a new job, a new friend, a new congenial group, a degree, a new love, a new skill, any of these sorts of things, or just success that comes from the steady application of your will and attention to some area of life, can have a positive effect on other domains.

Let's take another look at how the domains interact with each other. Due to the strong nature of the connection in Second Domain (Intimates) relationships, of course the First and the Second Domain affect each other strongly. Think of how the whole feel of an intimate group changes if one member is absent or a new member enters. New members can be excluded from true intimacy for a while, or taken in quite readily, depending on that set of intimates. Individual people and intimate groups, such as families, have varying amounts of tolerance for intimacy and varying amounts of time that they require to establish it. By definition, it does take *some* time to establish intimacy. "Instant intimacy" is nearly always false. A person must both know and be known for true intimacy to exist. A necessary ingredient of intimacy is acceptance, which can be there from the start, then grow in strength and value as the people come to know each other more completely.

> True in-the-moment seeing and accepting of another is one of the greatest gifts one person can give another, whether it is a new member of the family, or one we have known all our lives.

Most of us are probably more in the habit of thinking about how our Intimate and Group Domains affect us than how we affect them. It's something to consider.

As an example of how the Second Domain affects the Third (Groups), let's take the all too frequent scenario of a divorce, though of course there are times when such a breakup is the greatest good for the greatest number of domains. The people involved in a breakup tend to be very absorbed in themselves, their feelings, their reasons for and against the breakup, and so on. If there are children, hopefully they receive some consideration, but usually what happens is that that whole (intimate) domain as such misses being considered at all. A marriage breakup is not a simple loss, but a complex one. The two spouses, even the one who initiates the breakup, are likely to miss each other a great deal. The children will miss the parent they do not live with, or if they are shuttled back and forth they will miss the parent who isn't there. The conventional wisdom is that "children are resilient" and will survive the split. Of course they will. We generally all survive big losses and go on, though we often carry a burden of loss and pain with us.

To get the full understanding of this loss, especially from the children's point of view, however, let's look at what is lost to them. It is more than having both parents around on a daily basis; it is also the loss of the family dynamic as a whole. Never again will things be as they were. Even grown children who are off on their own or away at college will feel the loss of traditional family celebrations and holidays. While the younger children feel this too, the loss of these special times may pale beside the loss of the daily mundane pleasures of living together as a family.

Some people argue that if the parents are fighting and unhappy, the children are better off for the breakup. While this is no doubt true in some cases, proof that this breakup is the best solution would be if most or all of the people involved could say that they felt happier and better off a year or two down the road from the breakup.

Some couples are able to break up, marry others, and maintain a true family feeling. It is hard work, all too rare, and well worth doing. Even in this ideal situation, where communication is maintained in all directions, it is hard on the children until the new group of intimates settles into being. The point of all this is that it is better to acknowledge the loss fully rather than trying to minimize it. There is a better chance for healing then. In an ideal world, couples who marry would agree to something much more important than a prenuptial financial arrangement in case they divorce. This agreement would be to maintain all the aspects of communion and, if they must part at some time, to part as friends. It takes two, and probably some group support as well, to carry thorough on such a level of commitment. It's an ideal to aim for. Anything less leaves the people involved with baggage they carry away, either until they work it through, or for the rest of their lives. The evidence of that is the frequency with which family patterns repeat themselves.

Divorce also affects the Third Domain. If the relationship was truly poisonous in its dysfunctionality, the group the couple was part of will heave a sigh of relief that the drama (and bad drama at that), is over. In such a case, often the group had taken sides with one of the partners and the other one drops out of the group.

It's much more complicated if the couple has mutual friends who genuinely care for both people. There may be pressures from the combatants for group members to take sides. Even without that, there is the awkwardness of how to maintain both friendships. Primarily the loss occurs as the loss of that third domain *as it was*, with the couple as a part of it. In a real sense, the group as it was is gone. There will be considerable adjustment until a new group comes together and is comfortable.

Unless the couple has achieved the state of complete amicability, it's most likely that one or the other of them will end up excluded from the former groups they shared. It's just too painful to be with people you care about who are terribly uncomfortable with each other. Looking at this effect on the third domain (and the closer the group, the larger the loss will be), helps us to understand the outrage people sometimes express over a breakup. As members of second and third domain groups, we need to see the results of our actions, not just on the individuals involved, but on the group itself.

> Fully acknowledging a loss rather than trying to minimize it provides a better chance for healing.

Exercise 5-6:

Do a complete inventory of your domains, using the map you made before. List out all the parts of each domain. For each part:

- Take a good look at how each part is affecting you.

- Take a good look at how you are affecting it.

- What did you observe from looking at all that?

- Choose some action you can take, large or small, that will positively affect that area of you life.

Thoughtless harm and cruelty can come from a person believing that s/he cannot have an effect on another person or domain. Even if you believe that you have no power or authority over another person, you do create an effect on him/her in every interaction. We can see this kind of harm come about in relationships between children and parents, students and teachers, employees and bosses, or less obvious situations where there is an imbalance of power.

Exercise 5-7:

Think of some ways that a person who feels that s/he has little or no power can affect another (person or group) who s/he feels has most of the power in a relationship. Think of both negative and positive effects this person can have.

Now let's take a leap and consider how we as individuals affect our Fourth Domain of Humankind. The usual response to this is, "I don't!" or, "I can't!" but what if everything counts? This attitude of mindfulness, of "everything counts" has been rising for the past decade or so. Whether or not you believe that it is literally true, acting *as if* your individual actions affect the outer domains is a good guide for living. From the Fourth, it's not such a leap to think about how our individual actions affect life on the planet as a whole. In fact in some ways that may be easier to see.

The idea that the Fifth Domain, All Life, is so vast that we as individuals can't possibly have an effect on it does great harm. It's billions of people with that same idea that have brought us to where we are now in terms of pollution and imbalance with the rest of life on Earth. What can we really do? Besides giving our pets and domesticated animals good care, and looking after whatever bit of nature we have around us, we can be mindful of the needs of all life forms the world over. We can act so as to aid survival of all life.

Exercise 5-8:

Think of some ways an individual (short of being very rich and/or famous) could have an effect on the Fourth Domain of Humankind for better or worse.

Exercise 5-9:

Think of some ways an individual (short of being very rich and/or famous) could have an effect on the Fifth Domain of All Life for better or worse.

For the final leap, think about how your actions affect All That Is. This is "everything counts" to the nth degree. Most religions delineate which of your actions are acceptable to God and which are not. It tends to be a pretty one-sided relationship with the All Powerful. Whether you are religious or not, take a fresh look here. Imagine that your survival, your observations, your well-being, your thoughts and intentions count for something, right out to the far reaches of infinity.

Collapse and Inversion of the Domains

As a child's awareness develops, s/he moves from thinking that the universe = self to being aware of others. As the child continues to differentiate self from others, consciousness opens out along the domains. Obviously some people don't make it too far in terms of real differentiation and hence of understanding cause and effect in their relationships.[5] It's the work of a lifetime (or maybe several) to get fully aware and causative out through all of the domains.

---

[5] Three books shed a lot of light on development and differentiation. I highly recommend Schnarch, *Passionate Marriage*, 1998 on the subject of differentiation; Weinhold & Weinhold, *Counter-Dependency: The Flight from Intimacy*, 2004 on developmental tasks; and Karen , *Becoming Attached*, 1998, one of the best books I have ever read.

Besides all of the normal ups and downs in life, there are phenomena which occur when domains collapse or become inverted. This occurs when a person gives up on and retreats from the outer domains, collapsing inward. The retreating impulse comes as a result of unresolved losses, upsets and regretted actions. Finally we get, as someone pulls back:

- From the Third Domain: "My group against the world."

- To the Second: "My family (or me and my spouse) against the world."

- Down to the First: "Me against the world."

This person ultimately arrives at a not very powerful position. Cut off from the strengthening effect of good connections with the rest of his/her domains, huddled down into the First Domain, a person doesn't have a strong place to stand. Despite the non-viability of this position, it is glorified in our culture: the taciturn cowboy riding off into the sunset; the valiant woman going it alone without support. The fact remains, being in this "Only Me" frame of mind is not a good place to be.

From here, someone can give up on self and here is where things start to invert or turn inside out. He or she still has the urge to survive and to be connected with others. Only now, instead of coming from a place of wholeness, the person is hollow in the center, feeling disgusted with him or herself, and starts moving back out through the domains from this place of collapse and inversion. The things a person says and does in this condition may sort of sound all right, but they have a hollow, creepy feel to them.

An example of an inside-out Second Domain is a woman who lives for her family and through her children, but has no real life of her own and doesn't take care of herself. When her children grow up and leave home, she is devastated and feels she has lost herself somehow. An example of an inside-out Third Domain (Groups) is a workaholic who gives his all to his company. (There is nothing to say that the genders could not be reversed here, and often are. These examples just tend to be more culturally typical.) The workaholic pours his time and energy into his work, neglecting family and friends as well as his own health and well-being. Please note that both of these two stereotypical roles are well accepted in our society. (Japanese women's slang for a retired man is 'The Big Garbage', because he has lost his primary role in life.)

Inversion at the Fourth Domain (Humankind) starts to get a bit creepier. Here we have someone who will work hard on causes of social justice, but can't get along with the neighbors or his/her children or spouse. The old joke: "I love mankind; it's people I hate" represents a person with an inside-out Fourth Domain. Moving outward in this inverted fashion, we get to the Fifth Domain. Here you will find people whose attitude is that all plants and animals are good and all people are bad. In fact, we are animals too. Our species is a part of nature as well as any other, though it doesn't always seem that way. There is nothing wrong with a love of nature or a wish to protect and preserve the natural world. It is aversion to our own species that is the tell-tale sign of a collapsed and inverted Fifth Domain.

At the inverted Sixth Domain (All That Is) we have a person who preaches God and love, embezzles money from the congregation, kicks the cat and mistreats the children. This is about as far away from stable thriving domains as one can get. This application of this model explains previously difficult to understand human behavior. It would be all too easy to condemn such a person as evil. Though the effects of his or her actions might be evil, someone with inverted domains is still trying to survive. Gerbode points out that, in this inverted condition, a person is concentrating more on receiving effects on the various domains than on being causative in them.

This phenomenon is a powerful argument to those who tend to give and give of themselves without seeing to their own well-being. If you wish to continue to be able to give effectively to the people and domains that you love, you need to be strong at your center, rather than hollow. Taking care of yourself is a loving act toward your other domains.

What to do if we find ourselves to any degree collapsed or inverted? What seems to work best is to start at the center again, to work on strengthening and healing self, then gradually working our way back outward. As well-being increases on one domain, it starts to affect the others. For doing this work, choose the methods and techniques that support you best. As you know by now, I am a great advocate of TIR and Metapsychology, since I have seen them work so well for so many people. Whatever you use, I wish you success.

As we increase our survival across the domains out through the Sixth (All That Is), an opposite sort of phenomenon can occur. Gerbode credits Julie Grimes with the idea that strong connection with the Sixth Domain can cause an "eversion", allowing a person to reconnect more strongly with his/her First Domain, perhaps with realizations and greater ability to act, then the Second and so on. Once we get our domains into basic working order, we can pursue personal growth with enjoyment and satisfaction.

Decision Making as Informed by Domains

When you have a decision to make and the way is not clear to you, you can use your knowledge of the domains to clarify your choices. Should you accept a proposal of marriage? Change careers? Move to another city or country? Sit down with a piece of paper and write down which domains are affected by the decision you will make. Look at how they would be affected – pro or con – in each case and be sure to take into account both the physical and non-physical results of the decision. For instance, if you are contemplating a new job or career, will it be longer working hours than your present job, or shorter? How would that affect your First Domain? Your Second and Third? Will it mean more or less money? How does that affect each domain? Will it provide more or less job satisfaction? How will that affect each domain?

A man I knew had a very high-paying job with a chemical company. All of his extensive and expensive education had led him to this place. His family was delighted with him. Then he lost his job in an industry upheaval of "resizing". His family was aghast. How would he get another such high-paying job? He actually gave a great sigh of relief because though his job had been supplying him with material wealth, he had felt soul-sick for years about contributing to a company that he felt was doing harm. He found a group doing experimental farming to find new ways of practicing sustainable agriculture, where he could live very cheaply and work on something he really believed in. Not having any dependents, and not being very materially-minded in the first place, he found it easy to take a drastic pay cut to do work he loves.

I've found that even when a decision seemed difficult, once I start writing it all down as outlined above, usually one decision comes out as a clear winner over the other. Sometimes, of course, you just know which decision you want to make. In that case, it is unnecessary to employ this technique. This method of sorting through the potential effects on various domains is for those times when you feel unsure.

Exercise 5-10:

Think of a decision you will need to make soon, or in the future. Take a look at the domains that will be affected and how each option will affect those domains, both in the physical and non-physical aspects.

Lining up the Domains

There is a marvelous feeling when one's domains are "lined up", which is to say, united by fundamental purposes, intentions and principles, with each domain doing all right and contributing to the survival of the others. Interestingly, a life based on explicitly recognized purposes, intentions and principles is much easier to line up, domain-wise than one that's drifting along. Naturally, only you can say what those purposes, intentions and principles are for you. The stabilizing effect of knowing what you are going for, and what you are operating from, helps you to act consistently across your domains in accordance with the basics that are important to you.

The point again of all of this work is not to judge ourselves or each other harshly. Most standards of judgment and criticism tend to be pretty shallow anyway. It's not how much stuff you have, though stuff is nice, it's how many functioning domains you have, how well they are functioning and at what level of consciousness you deal with them. What really counts? You decide. I suggest for starters: personal integrity, quality of relationships, personal satisfaction, personal growth, and joy.

Exercise 5-11:

1. List out the fundamental principles and intentions that you use or would like to use to guide the direction of your life. (This step can take some time, work and possibly discussion.)

2. Take a look through each of your domains to see if what you are being, doing and having in each domain is consistent with your fundamental principles and intentions. Are there some areas that need work? Are there other areas that are already in line?

3. Take a moment and get the feeling of what it would be like to feel your life lined up and congruent with those things that you have decided are most important to you. How does that feel?

Exercise 5-12: Think of, or write down, what you consider would be the optimum condition for each domain to be in. The sky's the limit. Think big. World peace? An end to hunger and poverty? Humankind living in balance with nature? People building and manufacturing things in such a way that they will last for centuries, with people taking pleasure and pride in using well made things for generations? Every living person having access to all the education s/he would like to have? Everyone having the opportunity to pursue art, music, or creativity in some form? Think it, dream it, because as the Universe likes to say, "Thoughts Become Things." (See Mike Dooley's website: www.tut.com)

Chapter Summary

Mapping out our various spheres of influence and responsibility in the Domains model gives us a way to see life more clearly. The Domains include: the First, Self Domain; the Second, Intimates Domain; the Third, Groups Domain; the Fourth, Humankind Domain; the Fifth, All Life Domain; and the Sixth, All That Is, or God Domain.

Looking at achieving balance both across the physical and non-physical or spiritual aspects of each domain, and across all six, can give us insights on improving the quality of life.

Examining how each domain affects the others helps us in making decisions that will reflect the greatest good for the greatest number of domains.

The theory of how the domains can collapse and become inverted explains some aspect of human behavior that previously could be difficult to understand.

Thinking about your unique purposes in life can be useful for "lining up" your domains. When the parts of your life and what you are being, doing and having in each of them are congruent, you can see more clearly how to survive optimally in each domain.

6 Success

- Engagement in the Process of Living
- Understanding Success and Failure
- Using this Model
- "It's My Universe" and Other Views of Success
- The Danger Zone
- Drudgery
- Steady On: The Charms of Normal
- The Thrills of Success

Engagement in the Process of Living

The concept of *engagement* as defined by Gerbode sheds light upon many of the variables of life. Asking how engaged you are in some aspect of life is the same as asking how "into it" you are, how involved, connected and invested. In many aspects of life, there is a honeymoon period when things seem full of hope and promise. Engagement seems to come of its own accord during those times, which is misleading and potentially dangerous. No matter how automatic it might seem at times, our engagement comes *from* us, not from outside of us. Many factors can have an effect on a person's willingness to remain engaged, some covered in this book and many more addressed in the broad subject that is Applied Metapsychology.

The key point here though is that engagement is something you actively cause. The "it just happened to me" type of love or engagement has some element of restimulation in it. It is not a conscious creation in the present moment. Engagement (or love) that we continue to create is all ours and is subject to our will and our choices.

> Like love, engagement is something you *do*,
> not something that happens to you.

The dangerous idea I mentioned above, the idea that the state of engagement comes to us from outside without our active participation, is a trap. If we are effect of this phenomenon rather than cause of it, we are at the mercy of something or someone else to propel our lives in useful directions. (I am aware that the idea of this level of individual responsibility and causation might conflict with some people's religious beliefs. If this is true of you, I would ask that you read these statements as "creation" by the individual with, through, or by the agency of God.)

Taking over or re-owning the force of our own will to engage with things and people gives us a greatly increased chance of success in life. Using the material in this book may help to make that easier. This is true of anything that works for you: meditation, art, music, games, exercise, study, religion, communing with others in family, social, or work settings, for example. The fact remains that you have the ability at any time to invest yourself, to engage yourself in life or some aspect of it as an act of will and willingness. Traumatic incidents can blunt our ability to engage; so can upsets, regretted actions, and other factors. Doing our own work (individual sessions) is indispensable in my opinion, for optimum quality of life. At the same time, if we grant ourselves the ability to re-connect, to re-engage, sometimes we can simply *do* it.

Exercise 6-1:

- **Try getting the idea that you have the choice to move your own interest and intention (engagement) around at will. How does that seem to you? If you are working with a partner on this exercise, take the time to discuss this. If you are doing this exercise alone, write, think or observe.**

- **Get the idea that you can invest yourself in any area of life or any project that you choose.**

- If you were once strongly engaged in something and seem to have lost that, get the idea that at any time you choose you can re-engage yourself in whatever that is.

- Do this as long as you are interested or until you get a positive shift.

Exercise 6-2:

- Remember some times when you were fully engaged in something, a project, relationship, job, game, or whatever. Remember these in some detail, paying special attention to how that engagement felt to you.

- Remember some times when you became disengaged from or less engaged with something or someone. What feelings and thoughts accompanied this?

- Remember some times when you successfully re-engaged yourself in something.

- Think of some relationships, purposes or other aspects of life in which you have felt quite strong steady engagement for some period of time. Are there any particular thoughts of feelings that accompany those?

- Do this as long as you are interested or until you get a positive shift.

Understanding Success and Failure

Looking at the chart (Fig. 6-1) taken, with his kind permission, from Gerbode's book (*Beyond Psychology: An Introduction to Metapsychology 3rd Ed.*, 1995; see this book for more on the subject), you will see that at the bottom is "Final Failure" and at the top is "Final Success". Before we look at the *conditions* or stages in between, let's get a good grip in the concepts of Final Failure and Final Success. Starting a business will serve as a clear example of these. If you start a business that fails, eventually everything is gone. The group of people who were working in the business are usually dispersed, the money is gone, everything has had to be sold; it's over. Until that point, even if the business is just limping along, it is operating somewhere short of final failure. On the other end of the scale, final success, the business will have succeeded to the point where a larger company may come along and buy it up. If you sell your business, perhaps for a large sum of money, and turn over the reins to someone else, that is final success. Even if you stay on in some capacity working for the new company, you are not continuing the old successful endeavor, but really starting in a new one, as many who have sold companies have found out.

Both final failure and final success are endings. Both have a "Game Over" connotation and include disengagement as a component. Realizing this is essential for continued success in life.

> Getting stuck in either our old failures or
> our old successes can keep us from new possibilities.

Let's look at a marriage in the context of these definitions. Final success would not come until the couple had lived a good long life together and life was over. Until then they would be living success, but short of the ending of final success. Final failure would consist of the two people's hopes and dreams for a happy life together coming to nothing. In terms of the marriage itself, both the scenario of a bitter split and that of an amicable one fit the definition of final failure. Interestingly though, the relationship may still be good despite the two people deciding to end the marriage. While this is rare enough, perhaps it is becoming less so.

As an individual, there is no reason why a person can't reach the stage of success and stay there indefinitely. As long as you are happy with what you are doing, there is no reason to have to move on. The move to the Final Success stage comes when you feel, "OK, I've done that. What's next?" A superb musician may become a conductor or composer. A great cook might open a restaurant or write a cook book. A computer whiz might invent a new application. Despite the saying that, "Those who can't do, teach," often when people become masters in some field of endeavor, they move on to teaching, or include teaching or mentoring of others in their work. A dancer who can no longer meet the physical demands of dancing may go on to teaching, and may do so in the frame of mind of either failure or success.

Acknowledging the end of something, whether that end comes from our choice or is imposed upon us by outside circumstances, allows us to move on. A Final

Success can occur to us as a loss sometimes as much as a Final Failure can, even if it comes from a conscious choice we make. (TIR is good for resolving the pain of all sorts of losses.)

This brings up the crucial point that we're better off not adopting either our failures or our successes as definitions of ourselves. Think about the difference between saying, "My business was a failure," and saying, "I am a failure." It's an easy jump to make, but not a beneficial one. It takes some strength of character to admit our failures. If we call them whatever they are, a failed project, a lost game, or whatever – rather than a failed *self* – we are in a better position to look back and examine what worked and what did not, and also to move on from those endings into something that may be more successful. We're better off not adopting either our failures or our successes as definitions of ourselves.

What's wrong with being defined by our successes? What's wrong with saying "I am a success," when we succeed at something specific?

Exercise 6-3:

Think about this: Is there a downside to defining ourselves by our successes? What is the alternative? What advantages might it have?

"It's My Universe," and Other Views of Success

A good friend of mine noticed the tendency of human beings to act as if all of reality belongs to them. (When we do that, we are in effect collapsing our own mental-emotional-perceptual-experiential world with the "whole" world – the one we share with other human beings, life forms, objects and forces.) He would say, "What's wrong with these people!? Don't they understand? It's *my* universe!" whenever he observed himself or someone else acting from that "my universe" perspective. It's amusing to observe the outrage we sometimes feel when other people's perception of reality doesn't coincide with our own, which is, after all, obviously the right one.

There are two kinds of success:

- One is success in our own terms. From a person-centered way of working, that is the one we are most interested in. What did someone intend to achieve? Did s/he achieve it? That is the person-centered understanding of success.

- The other kind is success that is accepted and recognized by the outside world.

Both kinds can be very nice. The latter kind can lead, if obsessively pursued, to diminished quality of life rather than improved quality of life, due to the compromises one may have to make to achieve it.

Success on Our Own Terms

You only have to look about you a little to see that different people have very different ideas of what is acceptable, let alone ideal. I once knew a couple who lived happily together in what I (and I am generally thought to be quite a messy person) saw as incredible squalor. They frequently congratulated themselves on the nice home they had and how satisfied they were with life. From a person-centered view point, they'd have to be counted as successful in their living arrangements. A girl I knew won an Honorable Mention in a writing contest. Her friends thought that she would be disappointed not to have one of the top prizes, but she was delighted. Happy to receive the validation of the "Mention," she was so shy that she felt more recognition than that would have been overwhelming to her.

Exercise 6-4:

- **Think of a success you've had.**
- **What made it a success for you?**
- **Did other people share the idea that you were successful in that instance?**
- **Did it matter to you whether they did or not?**
- **Repeat as long as you are interested or until you get a positive shift.**

Success in the Wider World

The only problem with the purely person-centered viewpoint on success comes when someone wants something from the outside world in recognition of his/her personal successes (such things as fame, money and admiration being among the most common), and those things are not forthcoming. We are social creatures. We don't, most of us, seek only to succeed by ourselves. Writing a play that pleases the author is one thing. Seeing that play be a worldwide hit (if that is the goal) is another thing entirely. Why do we pursue goals involving the participation and co-operation of others when that can open us up to failure? Well, it does keep life interesting and exciting. Succeeding out in the world is a larger game, if you will, than pleasing only ourselves.

If we can acknowledge our failures and successes as what they are, we have a better chance of living to the fullest. Now let us look at the range of human endeavor where most of us live most of the time – somewhere between final failure and final success. The good news is that there are some well-tested strategies for navigating toward success.

Using this Model

Life is change. Just when you think you have command of some area of life, things can change and you find yourself in a new situation. Parenthood is a good example of this, as it requires constant adaptation. Or the nice small company you work for gets bought by a much bigger one. Or you get married and enter into a whole new life situation. This model lets you examine where you are and apply workable strategies to reach the condition where you'd like to be in that area of life.

We can be operating in different conditions in different aspects of life. That is important to note, because the tendency then is to wish to pay more attention to the part of life that is working relatively well and withhold our attention from the areas that are not doing as well. A woman might neglect paying attention to her marriage which is in trouble in favor of paying attention to her job where she is at a level of Normal or Success. A man might neglect his job which is in a condition of Drudgery in favor of an exciting new relationship. The neglected area of life is

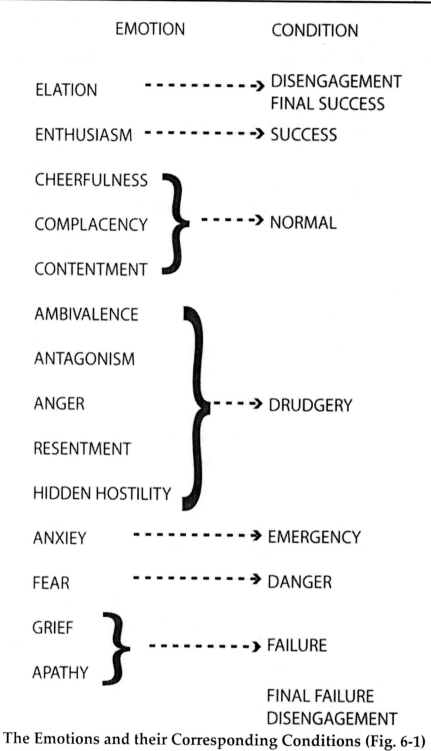

The Emotions and their Corresponding Conditions (Fig. 6-1)

likely to either stay stuck where it is, or to slide down even further. By the same token, one domain that is in a condition of Emergency or Danger can pull attention away from other areas of life that were doing all right, causing them to slide down as well.

Exercise 6-5:

1. **Think of a situation where one of your domains was in a much lower condition than the rest.**

What effect did that have?

2. **Think of a situation where one of your domains was in a much higher condition than the rest.**

What effect did that have?

Repeat as long as you are interested or until you have a positive shift.

The use of these strategies is meant for people who are capable of pulling themselves up by their boot straps. People whose lives are too chaotic or out of control are going to need some help at putting order and manageability back into life. Lower conditions can come as a result of outside forces such as disaster or famine, or can be predisposed by such things as poverty, lack of education and mental illness. Some people are in a state where they will need help and care throughout their lives. Others can, with a lot of help, reach a viable level of functioning. Some just need help to get out of an overwhelming immediate crisis. People who are basically getting by in life, even though things might be rough at times, can use this model to greatly improve life.

The Danger Zone

Before we enter into any new activity, we are on a theoretical null point in relation to that activity. We have not entered the game or invested ourselves in the activity. Wouldn't it be nice if we could just start any new thing into a comfortable position of Normal on the chart?

Outside, Looking In

If we make the mistake of assuming that we are at the Normal stage at the very start, however, we'll set ourselves up for trouble sooner or later. Just because a manager has hired us for a position, or someone has said that he or she will marry us, no matter how enthusiastic we are for the project, that doesn't put us into a Normal condition of operation. We haven't made the sometimes tricky leap from outside the game to inside as a full participant.

Negotiating that transition, especially when other people are involved (and they so often are, don't you find?) requires engagement, communication and useful strategy. The first necessary step is to establish good social communion with the other participants. You can ask yourself questions like these and then proceed to find out the answers through communication and observation:

- What does this person need from me?

- What does this person *expect* from me? (An especially important one if you are entering into a marriage.)

- What strengths do I bring to this position?

- How can I make best use of my strengths to meet the needs people have of me?

If it is a job situation, no matter how well-trained you were for your future tasks, you will probably find that every group, every company does things a little differently. As long as you expect that and are alert to finding out about these things, your transition into your new position will be much smoother.

This whole step is good to do again, even if briefly, if you have had a period of disengagement from the activity in question. If a long illness has kept you away from work, or if you and your spouse have split up for a while and are now getting back together, it's risky to jump back in with the expectation that everything will be fine. Paying attention to these getting-into-the-game steps will serve you well.

Danger & Emergency

Once you have gotten into the game, you need to handle any Danger or Emergency aspects of the activity. Moving up through the conditions is a very different experience than sinking down into a Danger condition from a higher place on the chart. Coming up from outside-the-game, one passes through the stages of Danger and Emergency often without a lot of painful emotion. As long as you are alert and still learning, you will get past the "Is this going to work? / Can I make the grade? / Will I be accepted?" fearful stage of Danger. The next stage is Emergency, which feels like anxiety, "Can I keep up? What if I do this wrong? Is this going to be OK?" Once past Emergency, you reach the relative safety of Drugdery.

Danger is a very stressful place to be, as it is down there far too close to failure for comfort. Examples of Danger situations are: a person about to get evicted, about to lose his/her job, about to lose his/her marriage. Most of us find Danger a pretty untenable place to be. There's an impulse to run away and let the relationship, activity, or situation fall into failure. If a person spends enough time hovering on the edge of Danger however, it is possible to get numb to it.

To get up out of Danger:

- Strengthen your engagement in the activity or relationship rather than withdrawing from the discomfort of the situation.

- Face up to any danger in the situation and handle it.

- Formulate any strategy needed to keep from slipping back down into the Danger stage.

That will take you up to Emergency, a less drastic stage than Danger, but still not a very comfortable place to be. At Emergency things are still not running smoothly yet. One's attention tends to be dispersed, trying to keep up with everything. To continue up through Emergency:

Renew your engagement.

- Make a list of everything that needs to be done and prioritize it, working with your partner, boss, customer or whomever, in order to make sure that key needs are being met.

- Carry on as above until you have the activity or relationship working on a routine, not an emergency basis.

- Develop effective routines and strategies for keeping the relationship or the activity on track.

> The emotions of anxiety and fear are much stronger usually if you are on your way down rather than on your way up the conditions.

Sliding down from a formerly good and comfortable position into Emergency or Danger can be painful. The outlines above for getting out of each of these stages and up to the next one still apply. If you are feeling overwhelmed in one of these stages, get someone to work with you and help to coach you through the steps.

After all this work, first to get into the game, then working your way up out of Danger and Emergency, your reward is arriving at… Drudgery!

Drudgery

To some people, routine life equals Drudgery. In fact, Normal is closer to routine in the sense of stability. As you can see in Fig. 6-1, Drudgery encompasses quite a range on the Emotional Scale, from Hidden Hostility up through Ambivalence. At Drudgery, a person has established enough workable routines to keep the whole thing going. If you are in Drudgery in relation to a relationship, or a job, or any other endeavor, you have enough of a grip on it not to be worrying about it all of the time, but it's not very much fun. Sadly enough, many people equate work with Drudgery.

Drudgery can be so dull that some people court the drama, intensity and risk of Emergency and Danger rather than staying in the relative safety of Drudgery. Since the emotions of the Drudgery stage are mostly in the anger/resentment band, a person in a job or relationship at this stage will tend to do the absolute minimum to maintain his/her position, and resent doing even that. The big mistake one can make at this level of operation, and one that's almost universally made, is to blame the environment for the Drudgery. The job seems to be intrinsically dull, or the spouse does, or the group of friends, or whatever. Housework can be done in a state of satisfaction. Brain surgery could be done by someone who experienced it as drudgery. As long as we consider that dullness to be imposed upon us, we are stuck. Once we take ownership of it we can do something about it.

To move up out of Drudgery:

- Re-engage yourself in the activity.

- Take action to make the activity easier by putting more order into the environment, honing you skills, or getting more training.

- Build communion with the other people involved. Handle past upsets and continue to improve your level of communion.

- If you can do so without getting overwhelmed, take on more responsibility, one piece at a time.

- Work harder than usual to produce more.

- Look for areas that need more attention in which you can be helpful.

Steady On: The Charms of Normal

Once up out of Drudgery and into the Normal stage, you can pretty well keep doing what you are doing, stay engaged, and enjoy the rewards of having gotten this far. The difference between Drudgery and Normal is like the difference between night and day. Drudgery is like plodding along in a trench. Normal is up in the light and air. Normal brings some room for creativity and new possibility. It's not necessarily all roses, but there is a baseline of OK-ness, of honesty, comfort and pleasure that is balm to a soul weary of the lower reaches.

A day in a solid on-going condition of Drudgery starts out rather blank and grey, or under a small black cloud. It's really not so bad. Nothing too horrible is likely to happen today; nothing very good either. Living in Normal, the day starts at least OK. There is some lightness and brightness to it. There is room for improvement and the real possibility that improvement is possible. A long-term condition of Normal will contain bits of both Drudgery and Success in it. The great thing about Normal is that it is maintainable as a good range of survival without heroic effort. Here engagement is not usually much of an effort.

It's possible to have made it to Normal, or even Success and slip back down into less desirable conditions. Traumatic incidents, losses, distractions, laziness, or substance abuse can disrupt our engagement and lead to a slide down the conditions. The answer for this is to determine where you have landed, apply the strategies for that level, and move on up again.

A life lived in a stable Normal condition with work, family and other relationships all doing quite well would have to be considered an enormous success by usual human standards! This would be a happy life. Even so, let's look at the steps a person in Normal can take to reach Success on this chart:

- Continue what you are doing that has been working well to this point.

- If some improvement of the situation occurs, observe carefully to find out what caused the improvement and if possible, incorporate this new thing into the normal routine.

- If something less successful occurs, investigate the cause, do what you need to do to remedy it, and develop a routine strategy for making sure that it doesn't happen again.

- Without dropping out any of your routines that are working well or disrupting your normal operating basis, try out some new plans. If they work out well, incorporate them into the normal routines.

Exercise 6-6:

Think of some examples, either from your own experience or from you observations of others, of each condition, from Final Failure up through Final Success.

The Thrills of Success

At enthusiasm, which is the emotional level of Success, a person is lighthearted, outgoing, adventurous and playful. The successful person is fully engaged. Though if you are at this level you are seen by others as being at the top of your game, you continually work at getting better at it, just for the sheer fun of it. You love what you are doing; you do it well, and you are getting the rewards for producing so well: usually financial well-being and the respect of others.

While Normal is good, even very good, Success is great. A person may reach Success in his/her career, relationship, or other area of life and continue there indefinitely if s/he uses the correct strategies. The steps for maintaining Success are similar to those for Normal, with a few crucial additions:

- Maintain successful actions and invest in that which will allow you to do more of what has already been successful.

- Maintain communion with the friends, supporters, and associates who helped you to reach success. This is a commonly violated principle.

- Meet all of your obligations, financial and otherwise. At Success, people often get sloppy at this, thinking that they have so much now that they don't need to be so careful. The opposite is true.

- If you are going to try something new, do so as described in the steps for Normal, as a pilot-project off to the side. There is a tendency to feel all-powerful, especially in the first flush of Success and to over-commit your resources (this is the reason that so many big lottery winners end up going bankrupt).

- Enjoy it! Share it!

The other possibility is that the activity will reach Final Success and it will be time to let it go. Gerbode notes that it is important to take time to celebrate those successes, but then to move on and re-engage ourselves in something new. Examples of Final Successes are: building a house, inventing something and seeing it through into production, raising a child who goes on into the world as an adult, starting a company and taking it through the stage of development (whatever that it) that interested you most, graduating from high school, graduating from college.

Final Success is often the start of a new activity. Success in dating can lead to finding a life partner, for instance. That's the end of the dating game and the start of the new enterprise of marriage. Ideally the partners will reach Success in this relationship before the couple embarks on starting a family, which is a whole new game.

In conclusion, these strategies are tools you can use over and over applied to various aspects of life. True happiness, personal satisfaction, high quality relationships, fulfillment in work, personal growth, all of these things are possible. These are much more possible when we have reached Normal or above.

Exercise: 6-7

- (Preferably with a partner) Take a look at some area of your life that is important to you and that is currently in the Danger to Drudgery range. Work out where you are in relation to that area. (Use the Emotional Scale to help with this.)

- Look at your level of engagement in relation to that area. Decide what you what to do about that. Re-engage as needed.

- Look over the strategies for the condition you find yourself in. Work out with your partner what specific steps you need to take to move up to the next level.

- When you are ready, look at the strategies at the next level up, etc. Do this if it inspires you, not if it seems like too much to look at right now.

- Keep a journal or some sort of record of your progress.

Chapter Summary

The chart in this chapter (Fig. 6-1) plots the various possible stages between failure and success against the Emotional Scale. The concept of engagement is the key to the attainment of success and to living life fully. Both extremes of Final Failure and Final Success contain the element of disengagement. Renewing our engagement at any of the stages in between can help us to move toward Success.

At each stage or condition from the bottom of this scale to the top, there are strategies that can help us to move upward. The bottom levels of the scale can be experienced as one moves into a new area or activity and gets established, or as one sinks down from the more viable conditions near the top. Sinking down into them is usually more uncomfortable than is working your way up from just having entered the game.

Danger and Emergency are unstable and uncomfortable stages. Drudgery is an improvement though it is still not a lot of fun. Normal is a real breakthrough into a viable and enjoyable state of operation, while Success can be the frosting on the cake.

Success is something that many pursue. With these strategies it is both easier to define and easier to attain.

7 Understanding "The Dark Side of the Force"

- Types of Negative Experience
- A Model for Understanding the Darkest Side of Human Behavior

Someone I once knew used to say, "There's a lot of sadness in life." Let us distinguish between the sort of sadness that comes along in the natural order of things, and another sort. The sadness a parent feels when a child leaves home, or that someone feels when a father dies, may serve as examples of the first kind. Since we live in the material natural world and natural disasters such as floods do occur and sometimes cause loss of human life or property, we can classify them as well with that first kind.

Now let us look at another type of sadness. While it may feel much the same, it has a different source. I am talking about the sadness results from human beings doing stupid and cruel things to each other. These could be avoidable sadness, were humankind in better shape. From my experience as a facilitator employing TIR, I have observed that traumas that come as a result of something accidental, traumas with no purpose or meaning, can be somewhat tougher for the client to resolve than those with natural causes. Hardest of all are the ones that result from deliberate cruelty or intention to harm.

Fig. 7-1 presents a rough scale of the relative difficulty of various types of traumas. There are many other factors that affect the magnitude of a trauma from one person to another.

"Natural order of things" losses: A child leaves home as a young adult; an elderly parent dies; someone retires; a family moves to another state, province or country.
Natural disaster types of loss or injury.
Senseless or accidental losses or injuries.
Loss or injury that comes from deliberate intention on the part of another.
Loss or injury deliberately perpetrated by someone we know or trust.

Relative Difficulty of Various Types of Traumas (Fig. 7-1)

Exercise 7-1:

- **Think of some examples of each of the types of traumas or losses in Fig. 7-1, either from fiction or from peoples' stories that you know.**

- **If you are working with someone, discuss what you have observed about peoples' abilities to deal with these types of events. What other factors affect their abilities to cope?**

Types of Negative Experience

This chapter deals with the last two kinds of experience in Fig. 7-1. These are the kinds of incidents which seem so very difficult to understand. In previous chapters we have gone over some of the causes for less than optimum human behavior: upsets (which can be hooked into earlier upsets), restimulated traumatic incidents, inversion on the life domains, and the lower reaches of the Emotional Scale. I would like to go beyond that and suggest a model that explains the worst and most hurtful aspects of human behavior. We might explain it in terms of a low chronic emotional level on the regular Emotional Scale, but in my opinion that misses a set of phenomena that this model explains more completely.

The Emotional Scale has been worked with, thought about and tested for years. It proves in practice to be a good solid piece of work. Let us start with that as a base, and then imagine that there is a mirror image of the same scale extending below it (see Fig. 7-2 on following page).

ELATION
ENTHUSIASM
CHEERFULNESS
CONSERVATISM
COMPLACENCY
CONTENTMENT
AMBIVALENCE
ANTAGONISM
ANGER
RESENTMENT
HIDDEN HOSTILITY
ANXIETY
FEAR
GRIEF
APATHY

POSITIVE

↑

--------------0--0--------------

NEGATIVE

⬇

APATHY
GRIEF
FEAR
ANXIETY
HIDDEN HOSTILITY
RESENTMENT
ANGER
ANTAGONISM
AMBIVALENCE
CONTENTMENT
COMPLACENCY
CONSERVATISM
CHEERFULNESS
ENTHUSIASM
ELATION

A Mirrored Emotional Scale (Fig. 7-2)

A Model for Understanding the Darkest Side of Human Behavior

In the center between the two scales in Fig. 7-2 is a theoretical zero line. Above that point a person is going about the business of living, with whatever degree of style and grace she or he is capable of. In fact, the majority of people seem to live above the line most of the time. Above the line, people wish for and strive for life itself and quality of life, not only for themselves but for their families and friends (indeed, for all the Domains within their awareness). So far, so good. There is room for human error coming simply from lack of conscious awareness.

A person living chronically near the bottom of the Emotional Scale can be enormously self-absorbed and not very aware of the effects of things he or she does or says to other people. The saying that, "Misery loves company," makes sense in that there is a tendency to want to pull others (either up of down) into the band one is occupying oneself.

For me, this was not enough explanation for truly horrendous human behavior, so I continued to read and study until I could come up with an explanation that made sense to me. Many previously inexplicable things fall into place if we assume that there is a mirror image scale below the original Emotional Scale, and that below the zero line the person's impulse toward life is reversed.

So, just above the zero line, we find an apathetic impulse to live and thrive. It all seems overwhelming and nearly impossible to a person who is living there, but that life impulse is still alight, even if it is flickering. Below zero, we find an apathetic impulse to withdraw from life or fight against it. The same pattern follows all the way up and down this double chart. In Grief and Apathy, a person is mostly closed in upon him or herself. This is true both above and below zero. Such a person is unlikely to cause huge effects on the people in his/her environment because s/he lacks the drive, focus and energy to reach out that far.

Once we get to the level of Fear, a person is at least looking about to see what might be threatening, and at Anger s/he is pushing out toward others. The antagonistic person tends to be a bit more light and playful than the angry one, and therefore more successful at engaging others in carrying out his/her plans. The cheerful or enthusiastic person is going to have the best chance of affecting others, because of the wider, clearer vision, ability and intention at these levels, as well as the charisma factor.

What happens as we move down beyond Apathy and Grief below the zero line? The same phenomenon occurs. Closest to zero a person has neither the energy nor the will to reach out much to create effects on others. As a person moves farther from zero, the willingness and drive to affect others expands.

The difference between Apathy on the positive side and the negative side is not huge, but it is real. A person in deepest apathy on the negative side of the zero line, can cause others to feel as though the light has been sucked out of a room that s/he enters. On the other hand, in our family we had an uncle who was positively an Eeyore of a man. ("Eeyore, the donkey" is a very pessimistic character, who takes the most gloomy and hopeless possible view of things in the Winnie the Pooh children's books by A.A. Milne.) We children loved that uncle despite the fact that he was too shy to talk to us, and we knew that he loved us. He was coming chronically from Apathy, but on the positive side of the scale. It could be frustrating to argue with him about the nature and meaning of life, but somehow it was fun too. We never budged him out of his pessimistic view, but we enjoyed the debates.

Understanding that the Emotional Scale represents a spectrum of emotion into which we could put many other shades of feeling, let us look at sympathy, which would fall somewhere between grief and fear. Things start to get really interesting this far from the zero line. Sympathy above zero is appropriate sympathy. If you feel rotten because you are ill, or because your sweetheart has broken up with you, your sympathetic friend makes you tea, lets you talk, says (sympathetically), "Oh, poor you!" (which is usually exactly what you want to hear at that point). S/he then carries on to cheer you up and bring you out of your miserable condition. Of course, on the positive side, Sympathy is not especially high on the Emotional Scale and could be annoying to be around. Sympathy below zero is another thing entirely. It may come at appropriate or inappropriate times, but its overall effect is always to make us feel diminished, enfeebled, altogether less well off than we felt before. Sympathy below the line tells you, "Whatever is going on with you, you are not up to dealing with it." It often has an undercurrent of gloating.

This illustrates the point that it is better to ask rather than to tell. This is why we use open-ended questions in person-centered work. Asking, "How are you?" (if you really care and want to know) is always better than saying something like, "You look tired," which has the effect of turning the other person's attention inward. Some well-meaning people go around making statements like that, but I suggest to you that it is a bad habit. If you want to be supportive, ask, don't tell. (Then listen to and acknowledge that answer of course!)

How to Tell the Difference Between Positive and Negative

It's possible to confuse the emotions above and below the zero line if you don't know what to look for. Tone of voice in Grief or Antagonism above and below the line might sound similar, but there are a few good ways of telling the difference. The intention behind the emotion really tells the tale. Let's look at Anger as an example. A person in Anger above the zero line may sound just as angry as the one below the line, but remember that his/her impulse is still toward life. Anger, especially the cold steely kind, is an emotion much glorified in our culture, probably because it is more alive and has more survival potential than the emotions below it. Take a look at some popular movies, especially action movies, and you will see that when the hero is moved to righteous anger, that is when s/he really gets things done. One key factor here is that the hero is appropriately angry. S/he has something real (within his/her frame of reference) to be angry about and once the situation is satisfactorily handled, s/he usually lets go of the anger. Anger is not *necessarily* a negative emotion. Focused and put to positive use, it can be very useful at times.

But now let's look at Anger below the zero line. Here we have the petty household tyrant or the boss everyone is afraid of. Around this person others "walk on eggshells", trying not to do something that will set him/her off (not that that can be prevented). This person leaves enormous destruction in his/her wake. So here we find one of the clearest points of distinction between emotional states above and below the line.

> Above the line a person's actions, fueled by the impulse toward life, tend to be more beneficial than not. Below the line where a person is driven by an impulse away from life, actions tend to be negative in their effects.

In differentiating between positive and negative, looking for the intention behind the emotion itself, watch closely. Generally, unless the person is too oblivious to even notice the effects s/he creates, you will see someone below zero manifest some small pleasure or excitement when s/he says or does something hurtful toward another and the arrow hits home. Someone above zero, except perhaps at Hidden Hostility, usually shows at least a hint of remorse upon seeing that s/he has hurt another. As Robert Rich, Ph.D. points out:

> "In domestic violence, there is a well-known cycle that includes remorse, shame, and genuine intention to avoid repetition. However, during the self-justifying, violent stage of the cycle, the person would definitely be below the line."

It's hard at first for someone above zero to see how anyone could be cheerful or enthusiastic below the line. In fact, self-justifying negative emotions are very energizing. Here is where we find the quite rare phenomenon of the "mad scientist" or dictator who wants to rule the world by any means, or someone who derives actual pleasure from hurting other living creatures, human or animal. It is, in fact, not easy to look at this. Organisms in general, not just humans, hold on to life as strongly as they are able. We cherish and celebrate the impulse toward life. Observing the impulse *against* life may cause us to feel frightened, threatened, queasy, or otherwise distressed. At the same time, there is a fascination in many people to look at or read about such things, probably in an attempt to understand something so foreign-seeming (compared with that impulse toward life) as to be shocking. If this fascination did not exist, we would not be shown so many grizzly things on the evening news, nor would "true crime" books sell as well as they do.

Exercise 7-1:

- Discuss (or write about) examples you have seen or read about of various emotions above and below zero.

- As you may have practiced observing various Emotional Scale levels and manifestations in Chapter Three, observe real life instances of emotion coming from the negative side of the scale. You may observe flashes of this sort of thing occasionally from someone who normally lives above the line.

The emotions we understand well are in a band right around our own chronic emotional level. Confronting strong emotions or actions coming from significantly below the zero line makes most of us very uncomfortable. Because of this, a person living well below the line has a disproportionate influence on his or her surroundings. We all drop down below the line from time to time. (Have you ever really wanted, even if only for a moment, to kill or hurt another?) Habitual criminals, whether or not they are caught, live below the line. Lack of understanding of these phenomena, means that criminally minded people are neither seen nor understood in their motivations and actions. Explaining away behavior that is against life, though a common strategy, solves nothing while allowing negative behavior to run rampant. For example, "he/she must have had a bad childhood."

Within a person-centered context, I am using "against life" in the broadest possible sense. One person might be against birth control and abortion, seeing them as an anti-life. Of course they are, for the particular life in question. Another person might see access to birth control and abortion as essential in the big picture: quality of life for each child that is born and quality of life across the domains. These are very personal decisions. We need to take care not to leap to conclusions about another just because s/he believes something very different than we do.

In Metapsychology we use different words in order to distinguish our work from traditional therapy. In Gerbode's view, as soon as you are talking about therapy or counseling, you have somewhat lost the true person-centered context. He sees the session work that we do as primarily educational in nature. (See his book on the Resource list for the full philosophical background of the subject.) So as I mentioned earlier, we call our practitioners *facilitators,* our clients, *viewers,* and the sessions themselves, *viewing sessions.*

In my opinion, one of the vital points of differentiation between regular therapy and the use of Applied Metapsychology in one-on-one sessions is that a psychology or psychiatric patient may be anywhere on this extended scale. TIR and Metapsychology are specifically aimed at and designed for people whose chronic level is above the line. The Metapsychology client may fall below zero from time to time, but doesn't live there. If the person's primary intention is to live and thrive, and for others to do so as well, viewing will usually work well. There may be some exceptions, but if a person has moved well below the line so that his/her primary intention is to resist and fight life, and to take others down as well, viewing is unlikely to be an appropriate method. The facilitator's intent to help that client to move in a life-ward, more survival direction and the client's intention to move in the other direction are at cross purposes. Rather than making assumptions about where a person is on the Emotion Scale, even if they are in prison or some other bad life condition, one can try some simple remedies with the person and see if they respond well to them. For example, TIR has been used successfully in prisons (V. Volkman, 2005). One of the primary tenets of Metapsychology requires that a person must enter into this activity willing to receive help. If someone is responding well to the techniques, then you don't need to worry about his/her being too low on this scale to make progress.

For a better understanding of this whole set of phenomena, read the fascinating book, *Inside the Criminal Mind,* (Samenow, 1984). It proposes a solution that has worked at least in some cases and could be implemented. Both *Inside the Criminal Mind,* and *The Gift of Fear* (de Becker, 1998) give fascinating insights into the thinking of a person who lives well below the line. De Becker warns that if we look at people who are capable of horrific crimes against others as some other form of life, we will never understand them. He also points out that people, whatever condition they are in, have many things in common: wanting some kind of connection with others, resisting rejection, seeking attention, and wanting control over their lives.

Another book, *Why They Kill*, (Rhodes, 2000), presents a theory of how a human being progresses to the point of being willing to kill another. It seems to be a quite precise series of necessary steps to bring that about. The author's intention in writing the book was to show how that progression might be interrupted before it is completed, saving someone from the consequences of that sickening slide downward. "Quality of life" for someone living chronically below the line is almost an oxymoron. A success for this person results in diminishment of the quality of life for those in close proximity, and ultimately for the person, him or herself as well. If we can face negativity we are less likely to be affected badly by it than if we cannot.

Finally, *Becoming Attached*, (Karen, 1998), gives insight into how a human being may be brought to inhabit a very low point on the Emotional Scale. We need to know and understand more. We need to be certain how to raise children to ensure them the best chance at mental and emotional well-being, not only for their own sakes, a good enough reason, but for the sake of our civilization. We need to find ways to heal severely damaged people if that is possible, or at least to maintain them in safety where they cannot hurt others – again, for their sakes and ours.

All of this is my theory. I invite you to observe for yourself and see what looks true to you.

Chapter Summary

It can be more difficult to face up to and resolve traumatic experiences that have been caused deliberately, especially by someone we know and trust.

It can be difficult to understand and to confront the excesses of human negativity that, though rare, have a disproportionately large effect.

If we postulate a mirror image scale below a theoretical zero line at the bottom of the Emotional Scale, it may give us a useful model for facing up to, understanding, and dealing with these disturbing emotions and behaviors.

| 8 | # Awareness Enhancers & Remedies |  |

- Communication Exercises
- The Orientation Remedies
- Conversational Remedy
- Awareness Enhancers

I have put these together because many of these techniques are good for both purposes. A note about end points in relation to Remedies: We generally expect much fuller end points from techniques used in a formal session, for a number of reasons. Remedies are used when something bad has happened as emotional first aid to help someone over the worst of it. The end point then tends to be as simple as a person's focus of attention moving from inward to outward or, the person says "I feel better now." When using a technique that could be used for either purpose as an awareness enhancer, look for an end point that is an actual positive shift in awareness.

Communication Exercises

These are excerpted from the Effective Communication Workshop (which has eight exercises), an introductory level Metapsychology training workshop.

The Communication Exercises given here can:

- Be centering, grounding, calming.
- Increase awareness if practiced regularly.
- Be useful in life for confronting difficult situations.
- Give similar results as meditation with more ease for some people.

Communication Exercises (CEs) are done with two partners seated facing and close to each other. During these exercises, you may notice that various physical and emotional sensations and feelings, sometimes unpleasant ones, will come up. The way to handle these feelings is simply to continue the exercise that turned them on, and as you continue the exercise, they will "turn off". It may be helpful, especially early in an exercise, to talk to your partner briefly about what is going on when one of these feelings occurs. Later, it is best to simply continue the exercise. But in any CE, be sure to remain in good communication with your partner. The point of the CEs is to have successes while doing them, not to achieve perfection. A success has occurred when you feel that, to a major or minor degree, you have:

1. Accomplished something.
2. Gained or regained some ability.
3. Experienced a sense of relief or release.
4. Achieved some kind of new awareness, insight, or realization.

An exercise is considered complete when you, your partner, and the instructor (if any) are all satisfied that you can do the exercise competently.

Communication Exercise 1 – Being Present

This exercise is intended to help you improve your ability simply to be comfortably present in front of anyone, with your attention in the present and without having to do anything. You are just being there.

In this exercise, you and your partner sit silently opposite each other with eyes closed, without talking, wriggling, twitching, or fidgeting. This does not mean you are supposed to be completely unfeeling or unthinking. But you should be comfortable just being present and being purely receptive, purely aware. Do not try to resist thoughts or feelings but rather simply remain aware of them without trying to change or affect them in any way. The point is for you to remain present and not to get lost in thought or preoccupied. Avoid using any system of being present. Just remain aware of present time and location and the person across from you. There is no complexity to this exercise. Anything added to simply being present comfortably in front of another person and being aware of what is going on around you is incorrect.

You complete the exercise when you can be present comfortably without becoming sleepy, going off into your own world of thought, or trying to do anything other than being aware of what is going on here and now.

On Confronting

"Confronting" does not mean "having a confrontation". To confront is to be able to face things (or people) without flinching or avoiding them, simply being fully aware of them, paying attention to them, being present comfortably with them, and not necessarily having to *do* anything to them or about them.

Confronting is the part of communication that gives people the most difficulty. Many difficulties would be resolved if people could comfortably face and be fully aware of each other.

Everyone has had the experience of talking to someone who is not confronting well. This manifests itself in various ways, such as a glassy stare, a vacant look, or shifty eyes. On the other hand, a person who is confronting well appears "alive", interested, and energetic. If you find yourself unwilling to receive someone's communication, it is better to make that clear rather than go on pretending to be there. When someone who is confronting well looks at you, you can tell that s/he sees you. You do not get the feeling that his or her attention is elsewhere when it should be on you. Such a person can put his or her attention where s/he wants it to be and can keep it there as long as s/he wants. S/he does not easily get distracted or preoccupied. Attention is not constantly turned inward onto thoughts and feelings but directed outward towards the environment.

Confronting defines a level of awareness, consciousness, and the ability to perceive. A higher state of consciousness or increased awareness minimally requires an enhanced ability to confront. Hamlet said, "To be or not to be? That is the question." The real question, however, is: "To confront or not to confront?" Each of us must constantly choose whether to be aware or unaware. Although it might seem more comfortable not to have to confront certain parts of life, problems are solved only by directly confronting them, becoming fully aware of them. Some people have the idea that if they do not look at their problems, the problems will go away. Of course, the reverse is actually the case. When problems are not confronted, they persist and accumulate. If you can improve your ability to face up to problems and to other people, there will be a dramatic improvement in the quality of your life. As a person's ability to confront problems improves, s/he becomes much less intimidated. It is worthwhile, therefore, to spend a fair amount of time on the two exercises given here, doing each one thoroughly.

When a person has trouble confronting, s/he often interposes something between him or herself and the other person and then uses that thing to confront with. For instance, if you are crossing your arms when you are trying to confront, you may be using your arms as an intermediary to do the confronting for you. It may not be a body part that plays the role of an intermediary. It could, for example, be an attitude that you are displaying, or some identity or role (such as victim or authority figure) instead of just being yourself and being there. Uncontrolled body reactions: wriggling around, fidgeting, giggling, laughing, having watery red eyes, excessively blinking and swallowing, are other indicators that a person is flinching instead of confronting well.

Real confronting is done directly from person to person, not by a body part or with anything else.

Communication Exercise 2 – Confronting

The purpose of this exercise is to improve your ability to be present while confronting someone. As in CE-1, you and your partner remain purely receptive, with your attention in the present. The only additional element in this exercise is that you direct your awareness to each other, face to face, instead of merely being passively aware.

Sit silently facing each other with your eyes open. Do not make conversation or try to be interesting. Simply pay attention to each other and say and do nothing else for a considerable period of time. When CE-2 is going as it should, you find that you feel relaxed and comfortable, with no inclination to speak, fidget, giggle, act embarrassed, fall asleep, or exhibit any other uncontrolled reactions. Normal adjustments in position and normal bodily functions like blinking and swallowing are acceptable, so long as these do not become a way of avoiding confronting or a sign of nervousness or discomfort.

Confronting in this exercise does not mean *doing anything to* your partner. You are not trying to create an effect on him or her, so do not try to be interesting or create any particular impression. Confronting is a purely receptive state. Simply pay attention to your partner, without doing anything else.

As noted earlier, confronting is done directly from person to person, face to face. You may find that you tend to confront using a body part as an intermediary, instead of confronting directly. Confronting with a body part can cause sensations or pains to appear in the body part being used as an intermediary. These negative feelings are best resolved by simply continuing to put your attention on your partner. When you do so, they eventually dissipate.

Sometimes, a person may use a *technique* of confronting such "confronting" by looking first at the left eye, then the right eye, then the nose, etc., by deliberately thinking about certain things while "confronting", or by using certain meditation techniques. These devices have no place in this exercise, because they make you less present rather than more present to the other person.

Interest

You will find that interest, which can be defined as "directed attention," has a great deal to do with doing this and other CEs successfully. Interest can be attracted by something "interesting" or repelled by something that seems dull or boring, but you can also consciously create and maintain your own interest in anything or anyone, without any external cause. When you deliberately and intentionally place your attention on another person, you will find that you have become interested in him or her, and both of you will experience a positive surge in the quality of your communication.

This exercise should be done using a gradient. The first time, you might do only one minute confronting, followed by a discussion. Then you can increase the time to five minutes, and so forth. Many students have done CE2 for periods as long as two hours with benefit.

The Orientation Remedies

This class of techniques acts to stabilize a person in relation to his or her body and environment, with a corresponding benefit of calming the mind. Have you ever had the experience of walking or driving somewhere in a state of anger or upset and arriving at your destination without having consciously seen much or any of what you passed along the way? As Dr. Gerbode says, "The mind is the first environment." When our thoughts and emotions are stirred up, they can take possession of so much of our attention that our physical surroundings seem dim by comparison (and such activities as driving are left on automatic pilot). The Remedies given below help to ground, stabilize and extrovert a person. (I am using the word *extrovert* as a verb to mean the shifting of a person's attention from being tied up inside, introverted and self-conscious to having his/her attention directed comfortably outward.)

These Remedies, along with those given at the end of Chapter Two, have the interesting characteristic of being useful at all levels of functioning. Anyone from a distraught, chronically over-restimulated person to a generally high-functioning, cheerful person can benefit from them. For any of these beyond the Large Object Remedy (Chapter Two), someone who is distraught may need the guidance and the encouraging presence of another person. Try some of these and notice what results you get.

Four Handy Orientation Remedies (or Locational Remedies):

"Look at that _____."

"Notice that _____."

"Touch that _____."

"Feel that _____."

You are directing someone's attention to objects (one at a time) by asking them to look at, notice, touch or feel the object you point out. Let the person you are working with take all the time s/he needs and wants to look at or to touch the object you have pointed out. You are inviting the person to establish his/her location in the physical world. As with all Remedies, you do this just long enough to brighten the person up. When he/she is more present and comfortable in the current environment and is satisfied with the result, then that is the end point of the Remedy for now. These can be done any number of times.

These remedies get much quicker end points with children. Be alert for the child's attention wandering or extroverting; that will be the place to stop. Always stop when a child (or an adult) says s/he is done. Pushing past the end point gains nothing, pushes the person back down the Emotional Scale and, especially with a child, will be likely to make him/her less willing to participate another time.

The possible uses for the Orientation Remedies are countless. Here are some examples:

- During a period of my life when I was undergoing quite a lot of dental work, it got so that I dreaded every visit. I would be tense and anxious and when I got the injection of anesthetic, my heart would start to race. I learned to do an Orientation Remedy on myself. I would tell myself to look at a wall; do that; then acknowledge myself for having done it. In a short time, usually only a few minutes, my anxiety would ease, my heart rate would calm down, and I'd be much better prepared to go through the experience. It could take longer to get this sort of result in some circumstances. The more often it is done, the better it seems to work.

- When my daughter Stephanie was a baby, starting from the time when she was only two months old, she would sometimes become very upset without any reason I could identify. Her father would carry her around the room and say, "Baby, look at that table. Baby, look at that lamp." And so forth. He would be very clear and gentle in directing her attention and would let her look at the object for a bit before moving on. You might see this as simple distraction, but I was impressed with his success in using this method compared to my attempts and those of others to distract her when she was upset.

- A friend of mine was working as a court reporter. One day a witness became so upset while testifying that she couldn't speak coherently. The judge called a 15 minute recess to allow the woman to compose herself. She went crying out into the hall. My friend the court reporter followed her out as it didn't look to her as if 15 minutes was going to be enough in the normal course of things. She went up to the witness and walked around with her, getting her to notice things until she was calmed down. The witness was able to finish her testimony all right after that.

- Another friend of mine had heard from somewhere that an Orientation Remedy could be used to sober up a drunken person, and decided to try it. He went to a park where a number of winos hung out. He found that it took very clean, strong intention to get an intoxicated person to actually look at a tree, park bench or whatever, and a great deal of patience and persistence, but he was able to do this more than once. I am not recommending this course of action to you! The recipients of my friend's attentions were irritated with him for causing them to sober up, as this was not the state where they wanted to be (which is another way of saying that this was not a person-centered application of the technique). Now they needed to find a way to get intoxicated all over again. I mention this example both to show the scope of this technique, and to give you this tool in case you every really need to use it. The use of this remedy in this or the following two examples requires an above average ability to be present.

- I once watched someone bring a young woman who appeared to me to be on the verge of a psychotic break into a much calmer state in about twenty minutes. To start with, she was talking somewhat wildly and gasping frequently, with her emotion rising and her sentences becoming more and more disjointed. The facilitator got her to sit down and sat near her. He said, very kindly and firmly, "All right, now what I want you to do is to look at this desk." She continued to talk and gesture, but he just calmly repeated the request until she did look at the desk. He got her to notice a number of things in this way, often having to repeat the instruction several times before she looked at an object. Once she was much calmer and no longer gasping, he said, "All right, now look at me." She did so, drawing a long, deep shuddering breath. After that she appeared to be much calmer and able to deal with whatever had lead her to be in that state.[1]

- As you might deduce from the above two examples, this could also be used in the case of a bad drug trip. I know of one instance when a young man took a hallucinogen by accident and was deeply disturbed by the experience. A kind friend did an Orientation Remedy for quite a number of hours. She knew going into it that this might be a long haul. It was very helpful, though in most circumstances an Orientation Remedy is fairly brief.

- The next example is kind of funny, though I certainly didn't think so at the time. My boyfriend's ex-girlfriend came to town and he decided to dump me and go back to her. He had the decency to come and tell me himself rather than letting me be the last to know, but then he did something really mean! He had correctly surmised that I was going to be very upset about this. He didn't waste time in trying to justify himself, or doing something really stupid like telling me that I should not feel the way that I did, in fact feel. Instead, he played the dastardly trick of using an Orientation Remedy to make me feel better! I resisted, saying, "I know what you're trying to do! I won't do it!" He calmly and kindly continued to ask me to look at the lamp without engaging in any discussion about it. Finally I did it, just to get him to stop pestering me. From there it was just a matter of time. Within a few minutes I was smiling and extroverted from my misery. Now I am not going to tell you that solved everything or that I didn't feel any more sadness about the loss of that relationship. Of course I did. But that was the only time anyone ever managed to break up with me and leaving me smiling, I'll have to say that.

---

[1] Please note that I am not advocating the simple Orientation Remedy as a cure all, or anything like it. A Remedy by definition is a technique one applies in a circumstance calling for emotional first aid. Remedies are not a substitute for needed medical or mental health attention.

- I have known both nursery school and elementary school teachers to use these Orientation Remedies to engage the attention of the children in their classes before starting the day.

Then and Now

This simple Remedy works by helping someone to get oriented in relation to time. While any of the Orientation Remedies bring a person more into the present moment, this one accomplishes it by directing the person's attention in time.

First, ask, "What happened?" Listen to the answer and acknowledge so that the person knows you've understood.

Then ask, "Where were you then?" Listen to and acknowledge the answer.

Then ask, "Where are you now?" Listen to and acknowledge the answer.

Repeat the then and now questions until you get to an end point, in other words until the person feels relieved and satisfied.

To illustrate the use of this Remedy and also the speed at which children can respond to these things: a colleague told a group of facilitators the following story. A few days before, his three year old daughter fell in the bathroom and hit her head somehow. She let her pain, unhappiness and need for assistance be known with loud piercing shrieks as she came into the living room. Her father was coming from another part of the house to help her when he got to the living room door and stopped, seeing that his four and a half year old son had already taken charge of the situation.

"What happened?" the little boy asked his sister.

"I fell in the bathroom!" she wailed.

"OK. Where were you then?" he asked.

"The bathroom," she said, crying more quietly.

"Good. Where are you now?"

"The living room," she said, no longer sobbing.

"OK. Where were you then?"

"The bathroom." (Sniffle.)

"Good, Where are you now?"

"The living room!" she said, now fully extroverted.

"Alright. How are you doing?" he asked, having correctly spotted the end point.

"Fine. Let's go play," she said, and off they went.

The whole took a matter of seconds. Recounting this to us, the father said that he might well have missed the end point, just because it came so fast. This story shows not only how quickly children respond to Remedies, but also how ready they are to make use of them.

Tell Me Some Place Where the Pain is Not

This works on the principle that pain tends to grab our attention and the more attention we feed into the pain, the stronger it can get, like a feedback loop. Directing a person's attention to areas of the body that are all right can be quite effective, and that is all you do, asking, "Tell me some place where the pain is not," as many times as it takes. Of course, as with the other Remedies, you are listening for the answer and acknowledging each time. My dad did this Remedy with me once while he drove me somewhere and I had a headache. I was very skeptical that this would work, but he coaxed me to try it. It took a while, maybe twenty minutes, with me saying things like, "It's not in my big toe." "It's not in the dashboard," and so on. Eventually that headache went away.

Conversational Remedy

This is the one that we all do instinctively when someone has suffered a loss, injury, illness, etc. when we ask the person to tell us what has happened. By listening interestedly for as long as it takes, and by making a safe space by refraining from comment, we give someone the time and space to examine what has happened and the relief of sharing it. You can encourage a person to say more in various ways. "Did anything else happen?", "Is there anything (or anything else) you want to tell me about that?", and similar questions can be used if needed, until the person has finished telling you. A few key points will give you better success:

- "Tell me what happened," is more gentle and inviting that the more abrupt, "What happened?"

- Listen with all of your attention. Don't add anything.

- Acknowledge when the person you are listening to has said it all. With a less verbally expressive person you may need to ask more questions to help get him/her through it, but if s/he is looking inward and telling you what happened, keep it simple; just listen.

- Once the person is through and you have acknowledged, in the likely event that the person still has attention focused on the incident you can ask, "Would you tell me again what happened?"

- Again, listen well and acknowledge at the end. You may repeat this step as often as the person is interested in telling you and until his or her attention extroverts from the incident you are addressing.

A friend told me an amusing example of this Remedy. (It illustrates again how children can pick these things up and apply them without a second thought when they see them used.) This guy was very tall and drove an extremely small foreign sports car. He pulled into his driveway after work one day and his three and a half year old daughter happened to be playing in the yard. Trying to manage several parcels as he got out of the car, he gave his head quite a whack on the door frame and yelled, "Ow!" His daughter (one of those bright, wild, rebellious children who happen to look like angels), came up as he stood leaning against his car, holding his head and moaning softly. With great presence and intention she asked, "What happened?"

"Well I was getting out of the car and I had these packages, and then I bumped my head right here…" He found himself explaining. This tot not only asked the right question, she was standing there perfectly still (a great rarity for her), listening intently, and did it so well that her father as we say, went right into session.

"Did it help?" I asked.

"Oh yes," he said. That picture has always stayed with me: the very tall man, the very small car, and the very small girl, using this Remedy with confidence and assurance.

There are more Remedies and many more short techniques that are part of Applied Metapsychology.

Awareness Enhancers

It is a cartoon cliché to have a large sign on an office wall saying. "Think!" (while someone is doing something ill-considered under that sign). Two better signs might be: "Perceive!" and "Intend!" Good luck with using these exercises.

The Communication Exercises are one of the best awareness enhancers. The first two of them, included in this chapter, are especially good for this purpose. In my opinion the CEs have the advantage over meditation because having a living person across from you, with and for whom you are doing the exercise, makes it a lot easier to remain present than if you are sitting alone with your thoughts and trying to be still. If you get a chance, do take the Effective Communication Workshop. It contains the same exercises that we use to train facilitators, but written with a view to using them in life rather than in session.

All Orientation Remedies are useful awareness enhancers too, if applied for that purpose.

Practices

• Practice really being with your loved ones a few minutes a day, giving them all of your attention, drinking them in, accepting them just as they are. Donovan & McIntyre (*Healing the Hurt Child*, 1990) ask parents in troubled families to give each child an undivided 5 minutes of attention per day. They have gotten significant results with this modest request.

• Now here is a challenge, do the same for yourself. Spend a few minutes a day (even one minute!) being with and appreciating yourself.

• Practice being aware of your co-creation of your living space, with the physical space and the arrangement of objects, the atmosphere, emotional level, relationships. If you live with other people (or animals), each one is creating part of this atmosphere. Observe how the parts flow together to make the whole. What is your part? Is it what you'd like it to be?

• Do the same with the culture of your work place. Observe all of these factors.

• Do the same for every group of which you are a part.

• Practice the exercises from the Chapter Three (The Emotional Scale) and the Chapter Four (Understanding & Improving Relationships)and any other from the book that you especially liked.

• Notice what makes you feel more alive.

• Practice predicting. Who is calling when the phone rings? How many new messages will there be when you open your email? How many times will your busy-body aunt tell you how to run your life next time she comes to visit? How many people will you be able to get a smile from in the grocery store today?

• Practice knowing. Give yourself permission to know things, such as what time it is before you look at a clock.

- Practice intending things: a parking place, a good day, the weather.

What is possible? Of what are human beings, individually and together, capable?

Exercise 8-1:

- **Think about what is possible in the realm of human ability.**

- **How far can we go?**

- **What abilities do we have that can be significantly strengthened?**

- **What abilities have we not yet seen that may be possible?**

Chapter Summary

Many techniques can be used both as Remedies, which is to say, emotional first aid, and also as awareness enhancers. All of the techniques are presented for use in a person-centered context.

Remedies help to calm, stabilize and orient a person in relation to the physical world, which in turn helps to calm the mind. Short periods of the Communication Exercises can be used as Remedies if a person is willing to try this. Of course the Orientation Remedies are good for all kinds of situations where a person is distraught or disoriented. Then & Now, Tell Me Some Place Where the Pain is Not, and the Conversational Remedy are all best suited to be used in a situation where a specific Remedy is needed.

Awareness enhancers develop abilities you already have, such as the abilities to be present, to observe your surroundings in detail, to extend your consciousness, and to cause effects in your environment. The Communication Exercises are excellent awareness enhancers. The Orientation Remedies make very good awareness enhancers as well. Finally, the list of practices listed specifically as awareness enhancers provide some ways to play with your abilities.

The more you practice with these, the smoother you will get with using Remedies and the more you will get from the awareness enhancers.

Afterword

The Adventure

In this book we have looked at some of the practical models and tools within the rich subject that is Metapsychology. I am grateful for the opportunity to share this work with you and I hope that you have found some new things to think about and some tools that you can use. Best wishes in the adventure of your life!

So far you have had a small sampling of what Metapsychology has to offer. I invite you to investigate it further. The TIR website: **www.tir.org**, provides a lot of information.

Human Potential

On the subject of human potential, I strongly believe that we have yet to see anything like the ultimate potential of human beings. I believe that that potential includes:

- The ability to live successfully, and productively, with satisfaction and delight on a daily basis.
- The potential to evolve in perception, ability, and wisdom.
- The capacity to expand our ability to co-create with others.

To see a short essay on what I think is possible, see **www.MarianVolkman.com**

Animal Intelligence

As I mentioned in Chapter Five, I have a great interest in animal intelligence and in inter-species communication. I am thinking about putting together a book on this subject if a review of existing works on the subject convinces me that I have something new and useful to add. For a brief essay concerning my initial thoughts on this also see **www.MarianVolkman.com**.

Appendix A	Glossary	

Affection: A willingness and desire to be close to, or to assume the viewpoint of someone. A willingness and desire to share experience or space with another.

Applied Metapsychology: The application of the philosophy of Metapsychology, often in formal one-on-one sessions, but also in other practical uses. The person-centered application of techniques designed to permit the viewer to examine his or her: life, mind, emotions, experiences (including traumatic experiences), decisions, fixed ideas, and successes, with the aim of resolving areas of charge and returning the viewer to a more optimum condition.

CEs: Communication Exercises.

Charge: Repressed, unfulfilled intention and the resulting feelings of effort, resistance, and painful emotion.

Communication Exercises: Exercises designed to improve each component of the activity of communication; used in training TIR and Metapsychology facilitators and also for improving communication skills for use in daily life.

Communion: A combination of communication, comprehension and affection. An increase in any of the three components tends to result in an increase in the other two. A sudden drop in one of the three components causes a drop in the other two and communion itself. This we call an *upset*.

Comprehension: The sharing of experience that occurs when communication is successful. It need not involve agreement or concurrence. Common ground or frame of reference.

Domains: The spheres of influence and responsibility that comprise one's life. The six Domains are 1. Self, 2. Intimates, 3. Groups, 4. Humankind, 5. All Life, 6. God, Infinity, All That Is, ... **See Fig 5-1 (p. 80)**

End Point (EP): The point at which a viewing technique (or other activity) is completed. In viewing it consists of extroversion of the viewer's attention, positive emotional response, and often a realization of some kind.

Extrovert/Extroversion: An extrovert is one who is social and outward looking. We have turned this into a verb to express the action of a person's attention moving from inward to outward focus.

Facilitation: The act of helping another person (viewer) to perform the actions of viewing. In order to resolve issues or to attain increased awareness.

Facilitator: A practitioner of TIR and Applied Metapsychology.

Introvert/Introversion: An introvert is someone who tends to be shy and withdrawn from people. We use it here as a verb to talk about a person's attention going from an outward focus to an inward one.

Metapsychology: The science that unifies mental and physical experience. Its purpose is to discover rules that apply to both. See also Applied Metapsychology.

Person-centered: Work that is based in the frame of reference of the client, rather than some external set of standards to which the individual is supposed to comply or adjust.

Remedy: A usually brief technique to assist someone in distress.

Restimulation: An instance of charged material, such as a traumatic incident, being activated so that the person feels effects from it, knowingly or unknowingly.

Session/Viewing Session: The period of time set aside for a facilitator and a viewer to work together toward the viewer's goals. The work is governed and supported by specific rules and protocols.

TIR: Traumatic Incident Reduction — A brief, non-hypnotic, person-centered, simple and highly structured method for permanently eliminating the negative effects of past traumas. TIR is part of the larger subject of Metapsychology. See www.TIR.org.

Triggering: the event of becoming restimulated by content similar to the original incident.

Viewer: The client in viewing session.

Viewing: The work done by the viewer in a session, looking at charged material in order to resolve the charge and reach a point of clarity and resolution.

| Appendix B | Resource List |  |

For information on TIR and Metapsychology see **www.tir.org** The website lists facilitators and trainers, gives details information about available training workshops and contains a lot of articles.

The following books and materials are available from the TIR website book store:

Beyond Trauma: Conversations on Traumatic Incident Reduction, 2nd Ed., 2005 edited by Victor R. Volkman – A rich resource of interviews and articles showing the broad applicability of TIR

Beyond Psychology: An Introduction to Metapsychology, 3rd Ed., 1995 by Frank A. Gerbode, M.D. – The textbook by the founder of Metapsychology

Traumatic Incident Reduction, 2nd Ed., 2005. by G French and C. Harris – Reference work for practitioners of TIR

The Table of Attitudes as seen partially in Fig. 3-3, showing typical attitudes for each Emotional Scale level across 20 subjects including: Ability, Control, Success, Perception, Rightness, Harmony, Truth, Relationship with Other, Relationship with Self, Wisdom, Identity and more. By Gerbode.

Bibliography

See my website at www.MarianVolkman.com and click on "The Book & Resource List" for brief reviews of all of these and other useful books

Covey, S. (1990). *The 7 habits of highly effective people.* Salt Lake City, UT: Free Press.
de Becker, G. (1998). *The gift of fear.* New York: Dell.

Donovan, D., & McIntyre, D. (1990) *Healing the hurt child: A developmental-contextual approach.* New York: Norton.

Golas, T. (1972). *The lazy man's guide to enlightenment.* Layton, UT: Gibbs Smith Publishers.

Goleman, D. (1995). *Emotional intelligence: why it can matter more than IQ.* New York: Bantam.

Gottman, J., & Silver, N. (2000). *The seven principles for making marriage work: a practical guide from the country's foremost relationship expert.* New York: Three Rivers Press.

Karen, R. (1994). *Becoming attached: first relationships and how they shape our capacity to love.* Oxford, UK: Oxford University Press.

Kasl, C. (2001). *If the buddha married : creating enduring relationships on a spiritual path.* New York: Penguin Books.

Keen, S. (1983). *The passionate life: stages of loving.* New York: HarperCollins.

Lorenz, K. (1997). *On aggression.* New York: MJF Books.

Pipher, M. (1994). *Reviving ophelia: saving the selves of adolescent girls.* New York: Putnam.

Rhodes, R. (1999). *Why they kill: the discoveries of a maverick criminologist.* New York: Knopf.

Rosenberg, M. (2003). *Nonviolent communication: a language of life: create your life, your relationships, and your world in harmony with your values.* Encinitas, CA: Puddledancer Press.

Russell, P. (1998). *Waking up in time: finding inner peace in times of accelerating change.* San Rafael, CA: Origin Press.

Samenow, S. (1984). *Inside the criminal mind.* New York: Crown .

Schnarch, D. (1997). *Passionate marriage: love, sex, and intimacy in emotionally committed relationships.* New York: Owl Books.

Sheldrake, R. (1998). *The presence of the past: morphic resonance and the habits of nature.* New York , NY: Crown.

Wallerstein, J., & Blakeslee, S. (1995). *The good marriage : how and why love lasts.* New York: Warner Books.

Weinhold, J., & Weinhold, B. (2004). *Counter-dependency: the flight from intimacy.* New Bern, NC: Trafford Publishing.

Woititz, J. (1992). *Healthy parenting: how your upbringing influences the way you raise your children, and what you can do to make it better for them.* : Fireside.

Wright, R. (1999). *Nonzero : the logic of human destiny.* New York: Pantheon.

Other websites of possible interest:

www.noetic.org – Website of the Institute of Noetic Sciences – Exploring what is possible in consciousness and evolution.

www.tut.com – Totally Unique Thoughts (TUT), the website of Mike Dooley & family – inspirational messages from "the Universe"

About the Author

Marian was born to parents who were interested in a wide range of things, especially the development of human potential. Exposed to interesting people having interesting discussions on this topic from a tender age, she grew up thinking that everyone had such discussions and such fascinating visitors at home. She had a shock when she moved away from home for the first time. University life was some sort of transition since study and thinking were at least tangentially involved. Out in the wide world, she sometimes felt like an alien.

She studied psychology, biology, and English literature, but then struck off on an adventure of learning. Marian traveled and studied with friends of her parents and friends of their friends, for an eclectic education all aimed toward discovering and developing the potential of which she felt sure human beings were capable. From the age of 21 she was using regression work (hypnosis and other methods) in pursuit of the goal to relieve people of the sufferings that seemed to block them from full use of their abilities.

In 1984, she met Frank A. Gerbode, M.D. through mutual friends and was immediately drawn to the subject of TIR that he was in the process of developing and to the group of interested seekers he had working with him. It felt like home. Since that time, Marian has worked extensively with Dr. Gerbode in the development of new techniques and in writing and editing new training materials for practitioners of TIR and Metapsychology.

In 1997, Marian documented her extensive training and experience in the field of trauma resolution and gained her Certified Trauma Specialist (CTS) from the Association for Traumatic Stress Specialists (ATSS). She has presented on various TIR and Metapsychology-related topics at many conferences since then, including ATSS annual conferences. She has been in private practice for nearly all of the past 36 years. She travels extensively doing professional training in the US, Canada, and Europe.

Her interests include: quality of life, gardening, travel, cooking, reading, telepathy, inter-species communication, and the nature of consciousness. She is married to author and publisher Victor R. Volkman and has one grown child, Stephanie.

She has a work of fiction in publication: *Turtle Dolphin Dreams* (2005) and has four more books "in the works" from Loving Healing Press (www.LovingHealing.com).

Index

Beyond Trauma:
Conversations on Traumatic Incident Reduction, 2nd Ed.

New 2nd Edition

"Not in 30+ years of practice have I used a more remarkably effective clinical procedure."
—Robert Moore, PhD

Victor Volkman (Ed.) takes the mystery out of one of the more remarkably effective clinical procedures in a way that can help millions of people revitalize and improve their lives. To those desperate people who have experienced trauma or tragedy, this process is a pathway to dealing with their feelings and getting on with their lives

In the new book **Beyond Trauma: Conversations on Traumatic Incident Reduction**, Volkman presents a series of conversations with a wide range of people from many different backgrounds and experiences. Each provides his or her perspective on Traumatic Incident Reduction, or TIR for short. The book explains the techniques used by professionals and patients to help people sort out, resolve and overcome the negative effects of painful suffering.

Readers will learn about how TIR has helped domestic violence survivors, crime victims, Vietnam vets, children, and others.

Praise *for Beyond Trauma*

"Beyond Trauma outlines the elements with clarity and insight as to how TIR will resolve wrestling with dilemmas, understanding your demons, and climbing out of emptiness."
 —Sherry Russell, Grief Management Specialist and Author

"Our staff therapist is finding Beyond Trauma very helpful".
 —Joan M. Renner, Director, Sexual Assault Program, YWCA of Clark County, WA

"Beyond Trauma is a recommended book for the professional or for the lay reader who wants to know about this technique before possibly seeking out a practitioner.
 —Harold McFarland, Readers Preference Reviews

"Beyond Trauma: Conversations on Traumatic Incident Reduction is an excellent resource to begin one's mastery in this area of practice."
 —Michael G. Tancyus, LCSW, DCSW, Augusta Behavioral Health

Loving Healing Press
5145 Pontiac Trail
Ann Arbor, MI 48105
(734)662-6864
info@LovingHealing.com
Dist. Baker & Taylor

Pub. March 2005 — 360 pp trade/paper — 7"x9"
ISBN-13 978-1-932690-04-0— $22.95 Retail
Includes appendices, bibliography, resources, and index.

For general and academic libraries.
http://www.BeyondTrauma.com

Traumatic Incident Reduction, 2ⁿᵈ Edition

By Gerald French and Chrys J. Harris

Traumatic Incident Reduction (TIR) explores a powerful regressive, repetitive, desensitization procedure becoming known in the therapeutic community as an extremely effective tool for use in the rapid resolution of virtually all trauma-related conditions. Replete with case histories and accounts of actual TIR sessions, this book provides a "camera-level" view of TIR by describing the experience of performing TIR.

"TIR emphasizes empowerment of the client; it is an excellent technique for viewing one's old trauma and processing them. This book is a superb description of the technique. It is a considerable contribution to the field of trauma therapy, and I have been enriched by this book."

—Shabtai Noy, Ph.D, Senior clinical and school psychologist, Jerusalem

"Wonderful ... French & Harris provide a wealth of information not only on handling clients suffering from known traumata and their sequellae, but also on ways and means of effectively addressing feelings, emotions, sensations, attitudes, beliefs and pains that have their roots in frequently forgotten incidents from the past."

—Alex D Frater, M.A.H.A., C.T.S.,
Former Vice-President, Australian Hypnotherapy Assoc.
Campbelltown NSW, AUSTRALIA

"Not just another technique for 'management' or 'assimilation' of intrusive trauma symptoms, TIR actually pulls PTSD, anxiety and panic disorders out by their roots, once and for all! In 30+ years of clinical practice, I've never known or used a more remarkably efficient and effective procedure."

—Robert H. Moore, Ph.D., Clearwater, FL

Pub. January 2006 • 200 pp trade/paper • 6"x9" • ISBN-13: 978-1-932690-06-4• $29.95 Retail

Loving Healing Press
www.LovingHealing.com

Printed in the United States
111352LV00004BA/97-100/A

9 781932 690057